"…all at once breaks a small light in the far West, a new world slowly widens to our sight… This new land is Photography, Art's youngest and fairest child…"

Royal Photographic Society Journal 1857

The relationship between Victorian art and early photography is an intimate one. It is no coincidence that many of Britain's first photographers were professional or amateur artists and vice versa.

My great grandfather Linley Sanbourne, the political cartoonist of "Punch" magazine, was a keen amateur photographer and used the camera to advantage for his drawings. As, of course, did Canaletto for his views of Venice and London, using a camera obscura, although there was then no means of chemical recording.

It was inevitable the early photographers would choose scenes already popular as subjects for paintings and sketches. The Bristol landscape provides a perfect example of this process.

The early 19th century Bristol School of Artists led by Francis Danby recorded the dramatic Avon Gorge, romantic Leigh Woods and the atmospheric streets of what had been England's Second City. A generation later, the photographers did precisely the same.

Many of these scenes remain almost unchanged today: we can see for ourselves how well the painters and photographers succeeded.

"A Small Light In The Far West" explores this fascinating subject by placing paintings and photographs of identical Bristol subjects side-by-side, allowing us to compare photography's first – and high-minded – attempts with those of established painters.

Snowdon

The Rt Hon The Earl of Snowdon GCVO

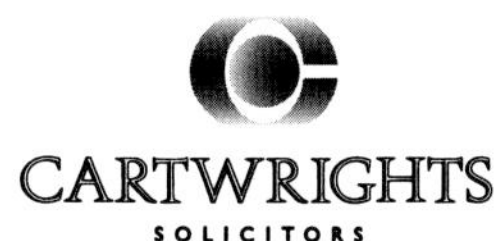

*Cartwrights is delighted to sponsor the exhibition
"A Small Light In The Far West", celebrating Bristol's
pioneering role in photography and our own close ties with
both Bristol and photography's early days. We are also
grateful to Bristol City Museum and ABSA for their
support of the exhibition.*

*Cartwrights was set up in Small Street in the old city
commercial centre in 1836, less than a year after
William Henry Fox Talbot's first successful photograph.
In 1840 Fox Talbot stood near our present offices to
photograph Broad Quay, including the Cork Tavern, which
was re-built soon afterwards as The Sedan Chair, now
owned by one of our clients.*

*Our founding came at an uncertain but immensely exciting,
forward-looking time in Bristol. Brunel, already at work
on the Great Western Railway, began building the
SS Great Britain liner in 1836.*

*Photography and Cartwrights went on to thrive together.
By the 1850's our practice was well established, whilst
Bristol's leading photographers had become known
nationally. Their achievements, and the debt they owed
to Bristol's landscape, should a be matter of great
local satisfaction.*

*Today, photography is universal and Cartwrights has a
national and international network of clients including
Marks & Spencer, Texaco, Bristol Airport and Bristol
Omnibus Company. We remain based in Bristol and take
immense pride in a city which is as progressive and
enterprising today as it was on the day we began.*

GEOFFREY JONES

March 1996

A
SMALL LIGHT
IN THE
FAR WEST

VICTORIAN PHOTOGRAPHERS IN BRISTOL

by James Belsey

An exhibition at the City Museum and Art Gallery, Bristol,
March 16 – April 21 1996

Sponsored by Cartwrights Solicitors

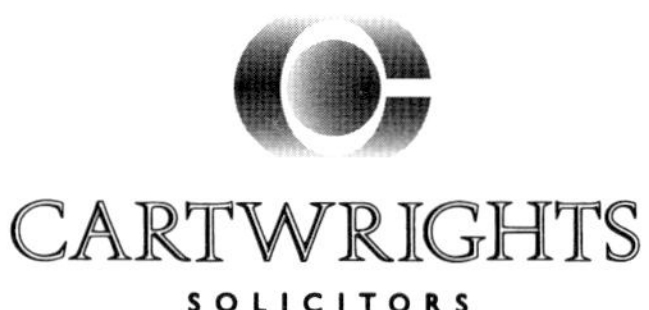

Published by James Belsey and Cartwrights Solicitors
in conjunction with Bristol Museums and Art Gallery

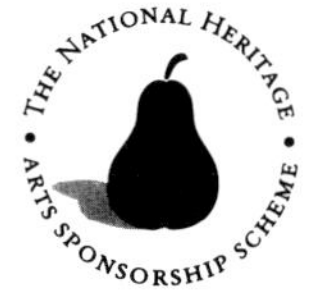

Contents

Introduction 1
City of Change 27
City of Artists 51
Art versus Photography 81
Acknowledgements 94
Bibliography 95

Typsetting by Parkway Graphics (Bristol)
Designed by Patrick Harrison
Printed by Triangle Design Print P.R., Yatton.

Introduction

Bristol has several claims to having played an important part in the history of early photography. But one aspect of its role has been neglected - the unique example the city offers of the link between 19th century romantic art and the first years of photography.

Bristol was where the first-ever recorded photograph of a ship was taken . . . the 1843 study of the newly-launched SS Great Britain when she was being fitted out before her maiden voyage. It is by the Father of Photography William Henry Fox Talbot who had travelled from his home in Lacock, Wiltshire to capture Isambard Kingdom Brunel's latest masterpiece of engineering on film.

What a moment. It marked the meeting of two revolutionary new technologies which would change the world as the first truly modern ocean liner came face to face with the new science of photography. That brief stab of light through a lens on a Bristol quayside simultaneously brought together two of the most visionary characters of the century, the ship's creator Brunel and photography's innovator Fox Talbot.

Today's global village spanned by cheap, efficient mass travel and linked by networks of mass media took another century or so to arrive, but the foundations were laid in that symbolic moment on the Floating Harbour.

Brunel's transatlantic liner cruised away down the Avon only to return as a rotting hulk more than 120 years later. Photography had come to stay and the city soon had a lively and sometimes very talented community of amateur and professional photographers.

They included the brilliant Hugh Owen, a well-connected Bristol accountant who created some of the most beautiful images of his day. He was a founder member of the very first photographic groups including the future Royal Photographic Society and took a keen interest in its rapidly improving methods.

Owen was an amateur photographer barely 10 years but in that time he took the world's first recorded photograph of a cornfield - quite a technical achievement in those days. He was chosen as one of the two official photographers for the Great Exhibition of 1851 and had bound volumes of his pictures presented to Queen Victoria and Prince Albert.

Another later photographer whose contribution is part of photography's history was William Friese-Greene, whose conservatory-like studio next door to the Victoria Rooms in Clifton still survives. The ensuing arguments over who really did invent cinematography will probably never be resolved but Friese-Greene has many champions. It is certainly true that he contacted the American Thomas Edison and sent him - probably foolishly - details of his newly-patented moving picture

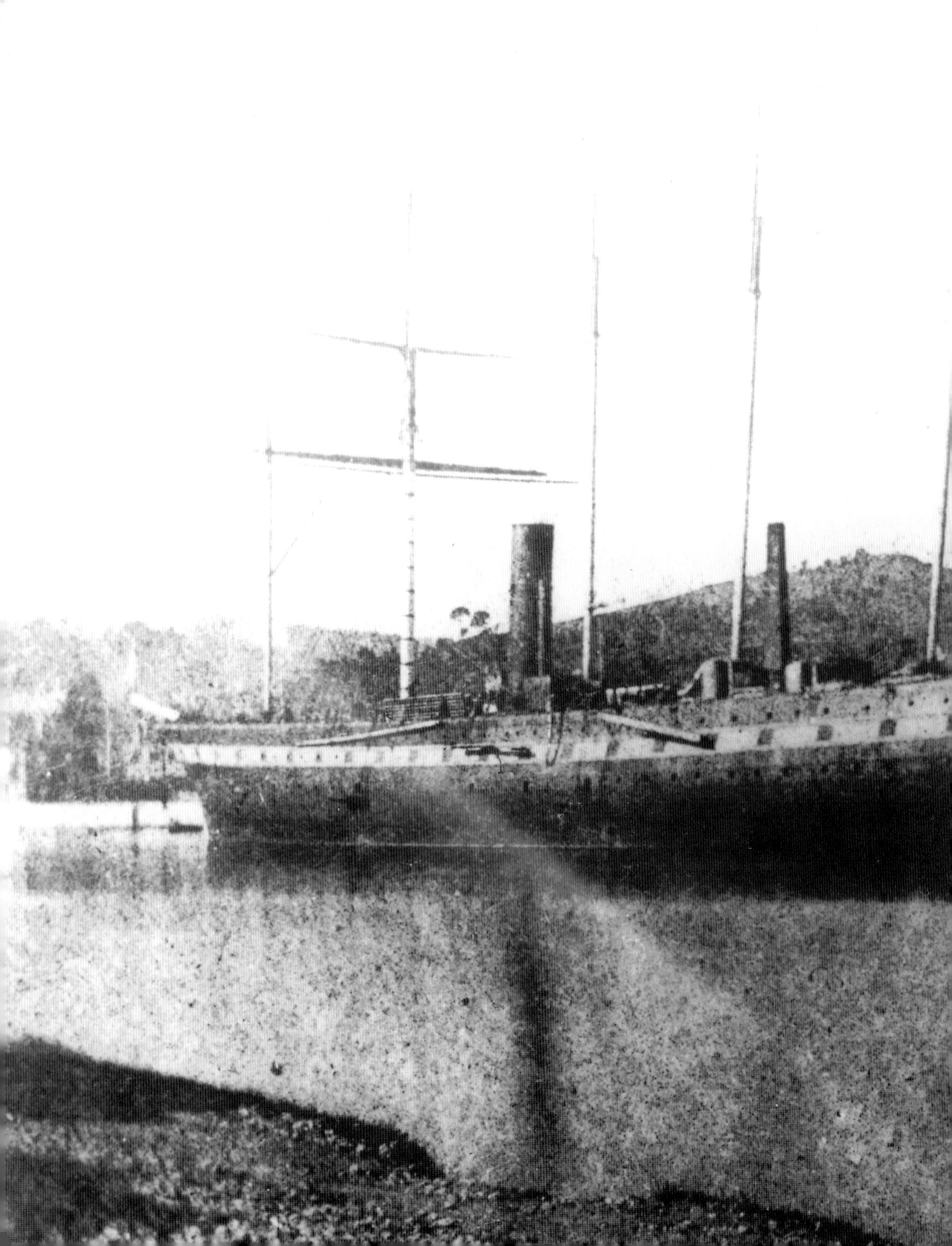

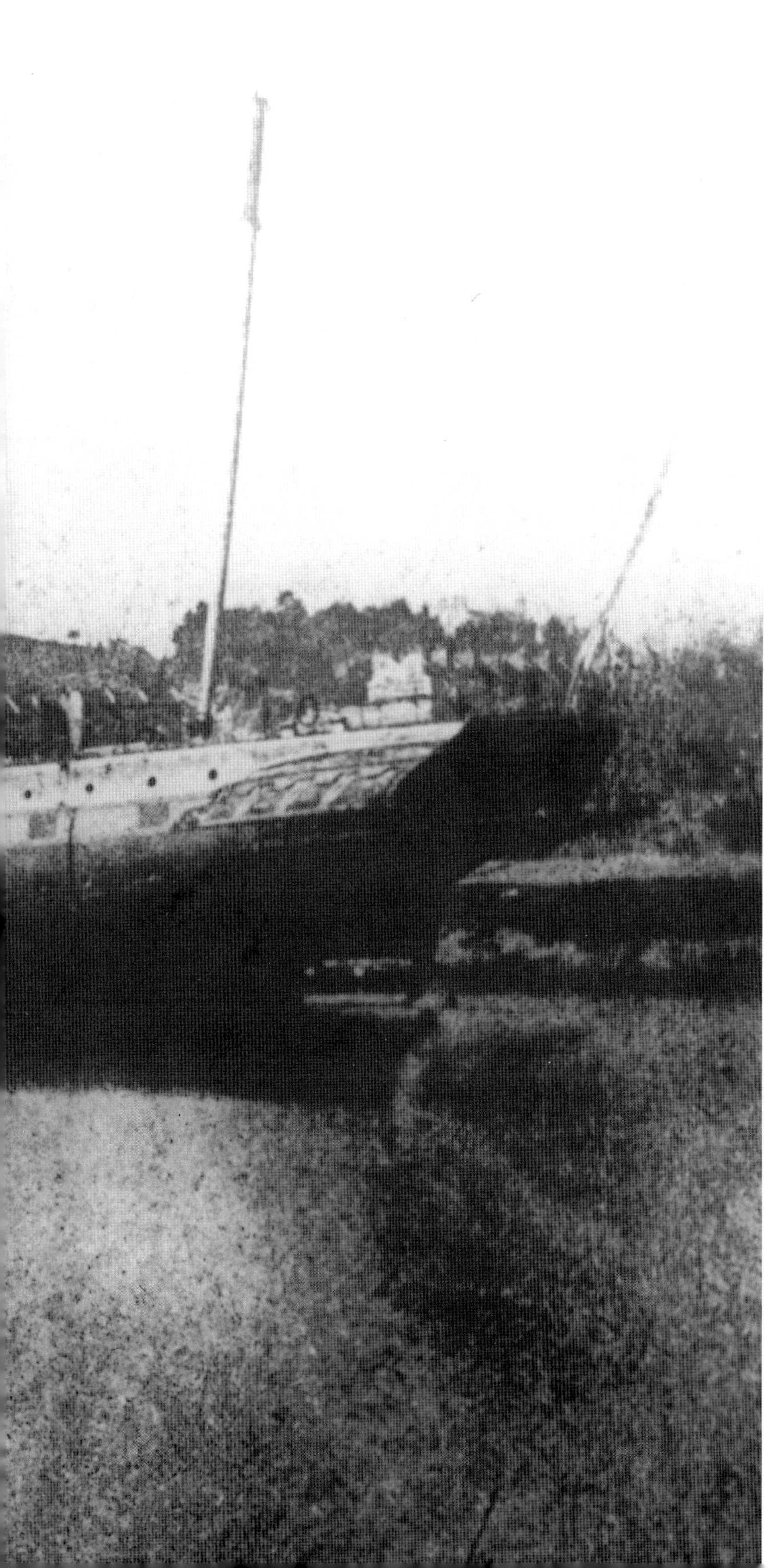

William Henry Fox Talbot's historic photograph of the SS Great Britain shortly after she was launched into the Floating Harbour in the presence of Prince Albert on July 19 1843.

Fox Talbot travelled from his home in Lacock, Wiltshire to take this picture of Brunel's magnificent liner as she was being fitted out for her maiden voyage. It is the earliest recorded photograph of a ship.

Fox Talbot's first known photograph of Bristol was a study of the city centre taken in 1840, just five years after he made his first successful negative at Lacock.

Photo: Bristol Museums and Art Gallery.

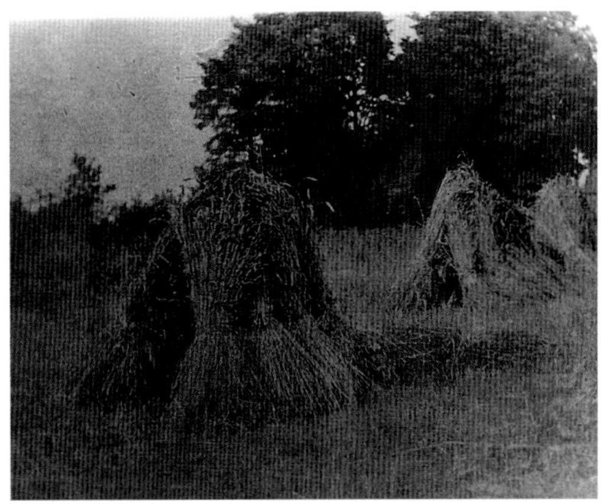

Hugh Owen (1808-1897), who took a very close interest in photographic processes and methods as well as the artistic composition of his pictures, was the first person known to have photographed a cornfield, a revolutionary achievement since early emulsions recorded yellow as black. The noted Bristol photographic historian Reece Winstone records frequent discussions between Owen and photography's founding father Fox Talbot on improvements in processes.

Photo: Bristol Records Office

process which used celluloid film with slotted edges.

Bristol was an ideal place to be a photographer. The pioneers were surrounded by scenes which had enthralled and inspired great poets and outstanding painters just a generation or two earlier. There was a wealth of subjects within walking distance.

Bristol had attracted some remarkable artists in the early 19th century, but reputations fade and tastes change. A century or so later they were largely forgotten until, in the late 1960s, art historians led by Francis Greenacre, Curator of Fine Art at the City of Bristol Museum and Art Gallery, began to research their work. Francis Greenacre's efforts demonstrated all too clearly that there had been a coherent Bristol School of Artists who had recorded wonderfully romantic subjects in the city's landscape.

Francis Greenacre's first exhibition on the subject, *The Bristol School of Artists: Francis Danby and Painting in Bristol 1810-1840* which was held at the City Museum and Art Gallery in 1973, caused a national stir and successfully established the School as a force in British painting.

This was followed by his exhibition *Francis Danby 1793-1861*. It was staged first at the City Museum and Art Gallery in 1988 and then at the Tate Gallery in London in 1989. Danby and his friends in the Bristol School have now taken their place in the history of 19th century art.

Bristol's extraordinary landscape lies at the very heart of the School's work. Danby, Samuel Jackson and their colleagues were thrilled by the sights which surrounded them. They came across wonderful medieval buildings, atmospheric streets and were confronted by the dramatic contrast between a busy, sophisticated city and the untouched, wild nature among the cliffs, ravines, downlands and woods which lie cheek-by-jowl with Bristol.

Early 19th century artists sought out and immortalised certain special views and places . . . the rugged drama of the Avon Gorge, the unspoilt glades of Leigh Woods and Nightingale Valley, the open Downs with their sweeping vistas of Somerset and the outlines of the Welsh mountains, the cramped streets and medieval buildings of the old city, the noisy, crowded, cosmopolitan quaysides of the harbour and the intimate rustic charm of the dappled Frome Valley.

In their turn the early photographers were an equally high-minded, artistic group who were inspired by exactly the same subjects. It was inevitable that they would follow, quite literally, in the footsteps of Danby and his friends to the places which the artists had celebrated so lyrically not long before. The cameramen wanted to capture that beauty immediately on film and the

Right: Clifton Rocks from Rownham Fields c.1821 by Francis Danby (1793-1861). The naturalism of the scene with its ill-shod boys, unkempt weeds and dramatic backdrop of oak-framed cliffs perfectly expresses the romantic appeal of the Gorge to painters... and, later, photographers.

Painting: Bristol Museums and Art Gallery

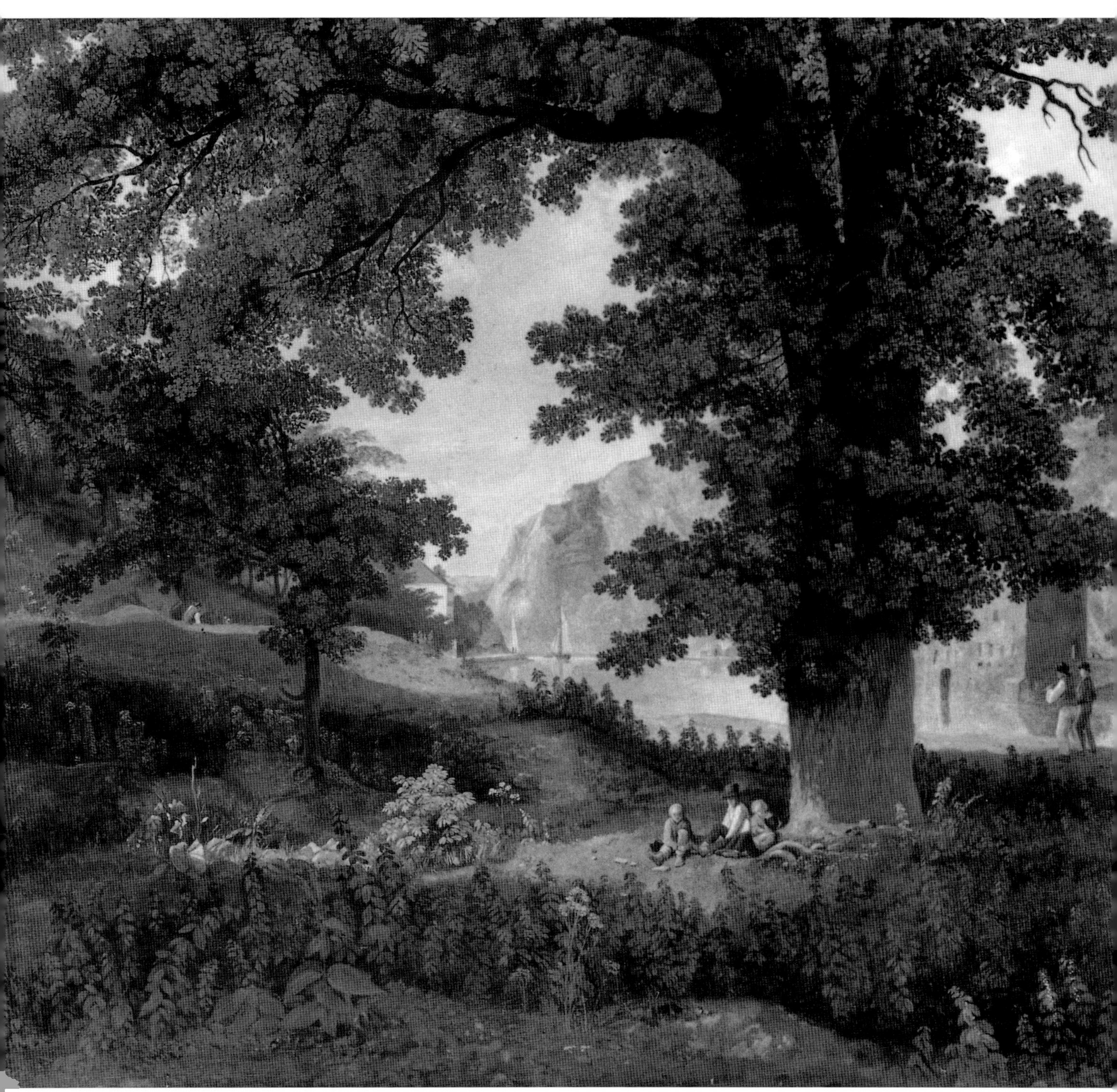

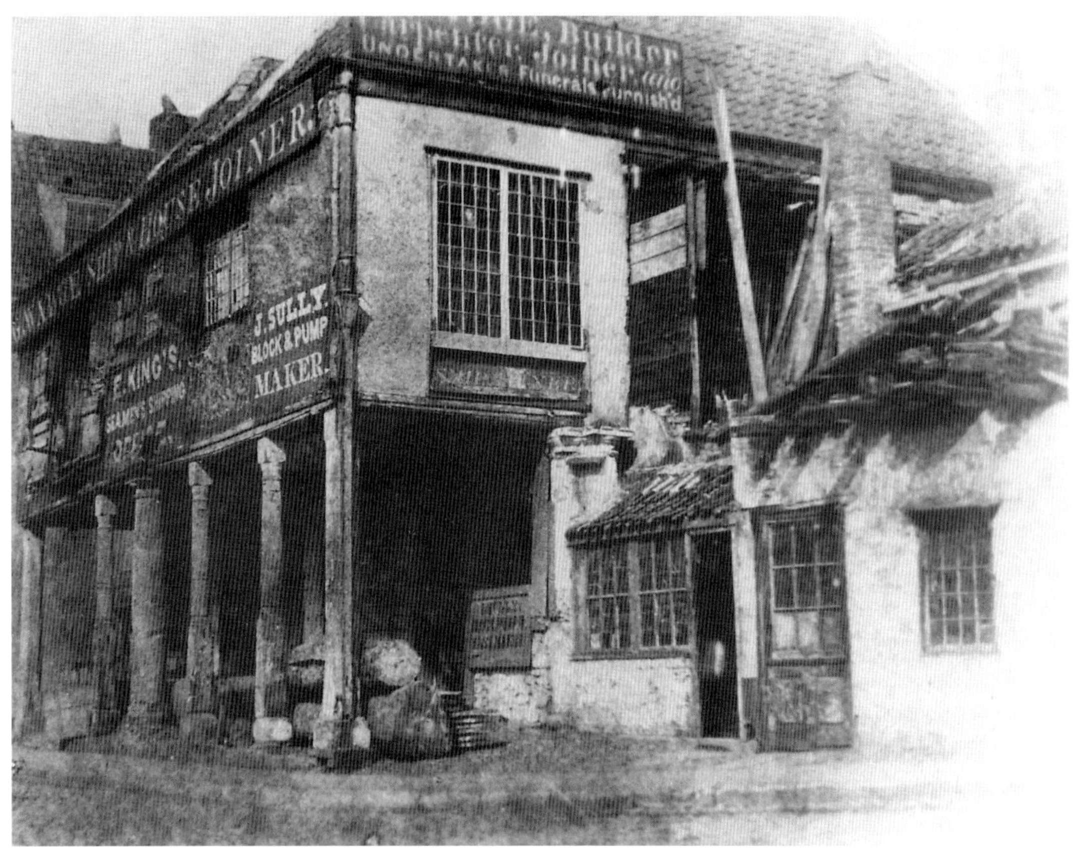

One of the earliest photographs of Bristol by Hugh Owen (1808-1897) is his study of tradesmen's shops in the 17th century Corn Exchange on Narrow Quay, which was demolished in 1849. By the late 1840s Owen was hard at work recording for posterity changing scenes in Bristol as well as the city's most historic sights and the beauties of its surrounding countryside.

Photo: Bristol Records Office

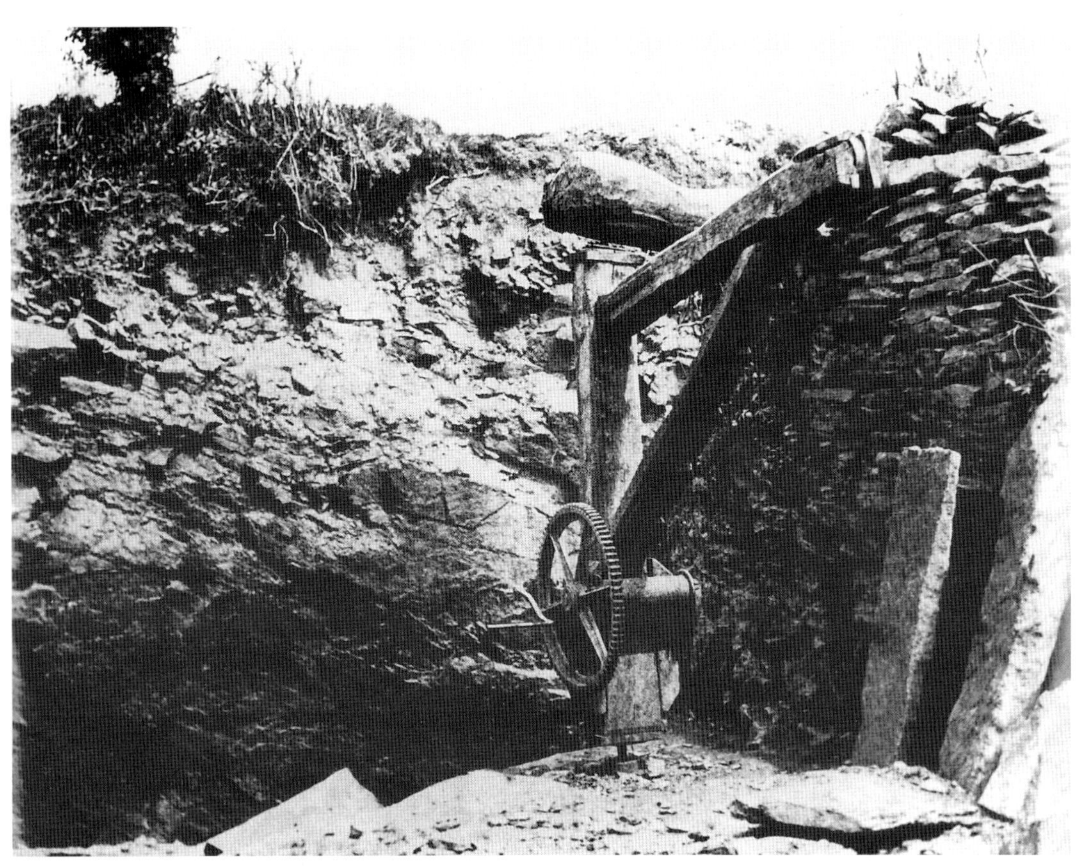

A winch in a quarry at Hanham, attributed to Hugh Owen (1808-1897). By the early 1850s, besides recording medieval Bristol, important buildings and the natural beauty of the Downs, Avon Gorge, Leigh Woods and Frome valley, Owen and his Bristol colleagues' newly attuned eyes were finding striking photographic material in subjects which very few painters would have tackled. Photography was already starting to teach artists a lesson or two.

Photo: Bristol Records Office

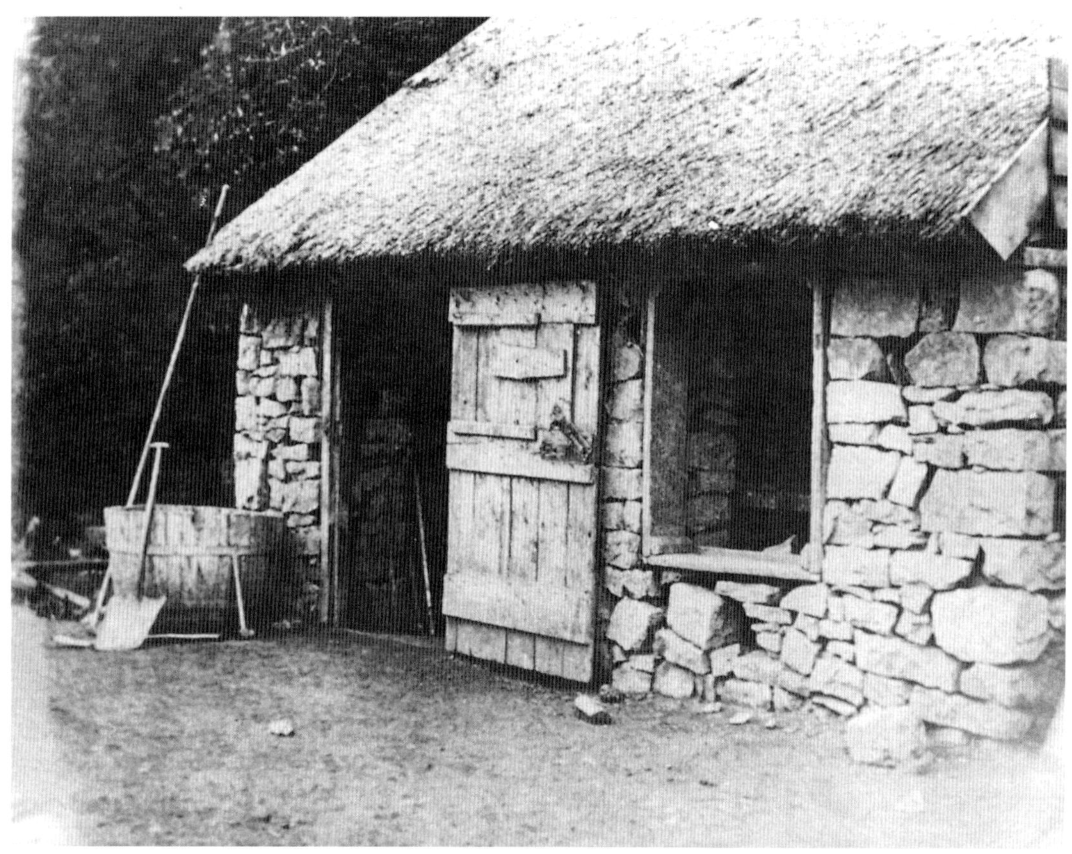

Above: The Shed By The Rocks is thought to be a shed at the foot of Sea Walls, then known as the Black Rock Quarry. The quarrying industry in the Avon Gorge proved a fruitful subject for early photographers including John Bevan Hazard.

Photo: Bristol Museums and Art Gallery

Opposite: The Blue Bowl in the Pithay in the 1860s with 'relaxed' group of bystanders outside. By now photographs of the picturesque streets of Bristol were beginning to feature people rapidly becoming accustomed to the stricture that they must stand still for a while if their images were to appear clearly.

Photo: Bristol Museums and Art Gallery

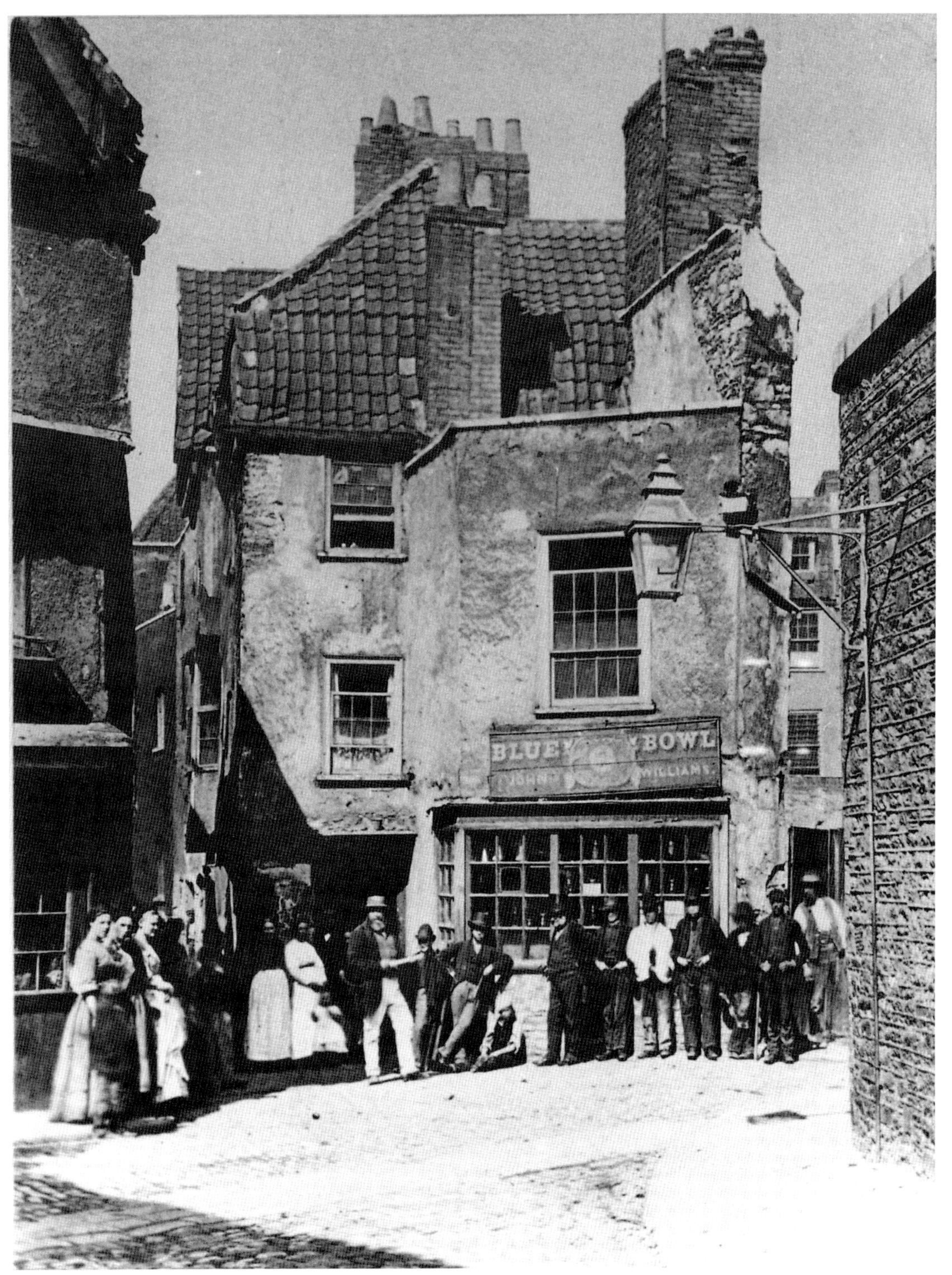

BLUE BOWL
JOHN WILLIAMS

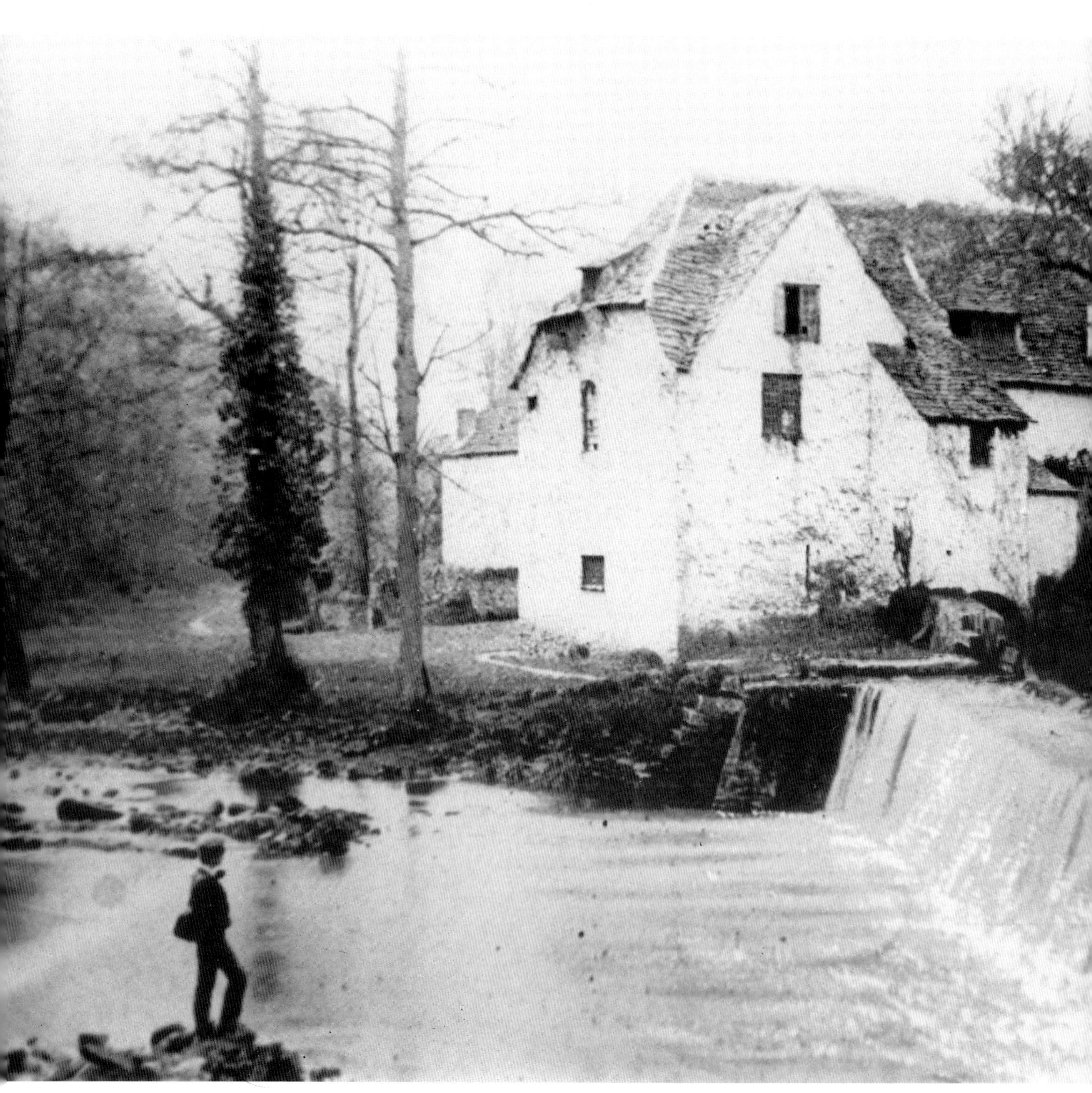

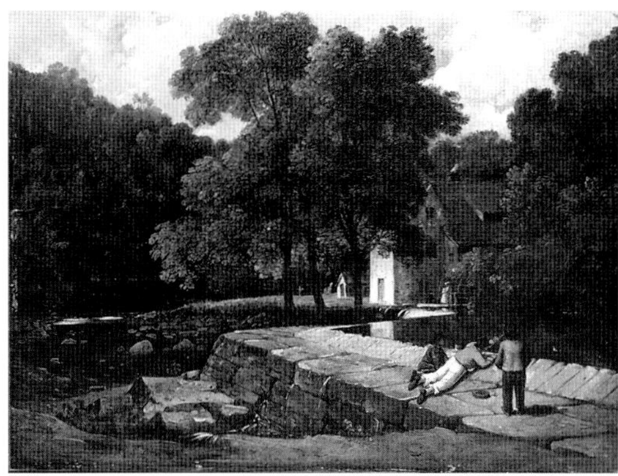

Stapleton Glen and the dappled intimacy of the wooded Frome Valley with its mill and weirs provided a charming contrast to the rugged, epic scale of the Avon Gorge.

Above: The Snuff Mill, Stapleton (c. 1822) by Francis Danby (1793-1861) is a delightful celebration of one of his favourite Bristol haunts. It was inevitable that the early Bristol photographers would emulate it.

Opposite: This 1850s photograph of the same scene again uses a child's figure to enliven a riverside landscape but this time seen in winter with the trees bare and the valley less inviting than in Danby's version.

Watercolour: Bristol Museums and Art Gallery; Photo: Bristol Records Office

inspiration Bristol provided was not confined to local photographers in those first days. At least three of the 21-strong founding Council of the Photographic Society - including Hugh Owen - had chosen the Bristol landscape as a major theme of their work.

Photography grew in self-confidence almost as quickly as the technological advances which transformed it from an uncertain, clumsy science into a thoroughly reliable, universal process. These first, sensitive pioneers who had been very self-conscious about photography's place in the scheme of things - the argument over photography's relationship with art raged at the time and still has its echoes today - were rapidly replaced by a workmanlike army of lensmen who'd knock off a set of portraits, visiting cards or postcards without a lofty thought in their mind.

The Golden Age of 19th century Bristol painting lasted from approximately 1810 to 1840. The Golden Age of Bristol photography was in and around the 1850s. By then the pioneers had mastered the limited technology and begun to express themselves, not only by celebrating the Bristol landscape but also by widening their horizons with well-made still lifes, interiors and even costume portraiture.

The most thrilling single collection of their work is in a leather-bound album to be found in the Bristol Records Office. The album, from the estate of Ellison Fuller-Eberle was presented to the city by his brother Victor and is one of Bristol's greatest treasures. It had belonged to the Fedden family of Redland. I can never forget the moment I first turned its pages and saw these masterpieces. It happened almost 20 years ago but I can still vividly recall the excitement of that discovery one dull, dreary morning in the 1970s.

That day's job was a routine piece of nostalgia journalism. I'd been asked to track down 25 or so nice old photographs for a pictorial series in the Bristol Evening Post. I could have gone in any one of a dozen directions - to the City Museum, to local postcard-collecting clubs or to Reece Winstone, the magpie-like collector and publisher of old Bristol photographs. Instead, luckily, Bristol City Council's press office put me in touch with Bristol Records Office.

Yes, they said, they had some interesting old pictures which might fit the bill. I walked across from the Evening Post's offices on Temple Way to the Council House, where the Records Office used to be in those days.

There, one of the staff came forward bearing a large, heavy volume which she placed on the table and carefully untied the ribbon with its reference number. She left me alone to get to work.

I had been expecting cheerful, lively sepia Victorian or Edwardian street scenes with funny old vehicles, chaps in top hats, girls and women in big dresses. . . all the standard "Dickensian" fare of workmanlike 19th or early 20th century photography.

What I found were a sequence of enchanting images in the silent hour or so it took me to turn the pages back and forward, revisiting instant favourites or moving ahead to new discoveries.

There were still, frozen studies of an eerie

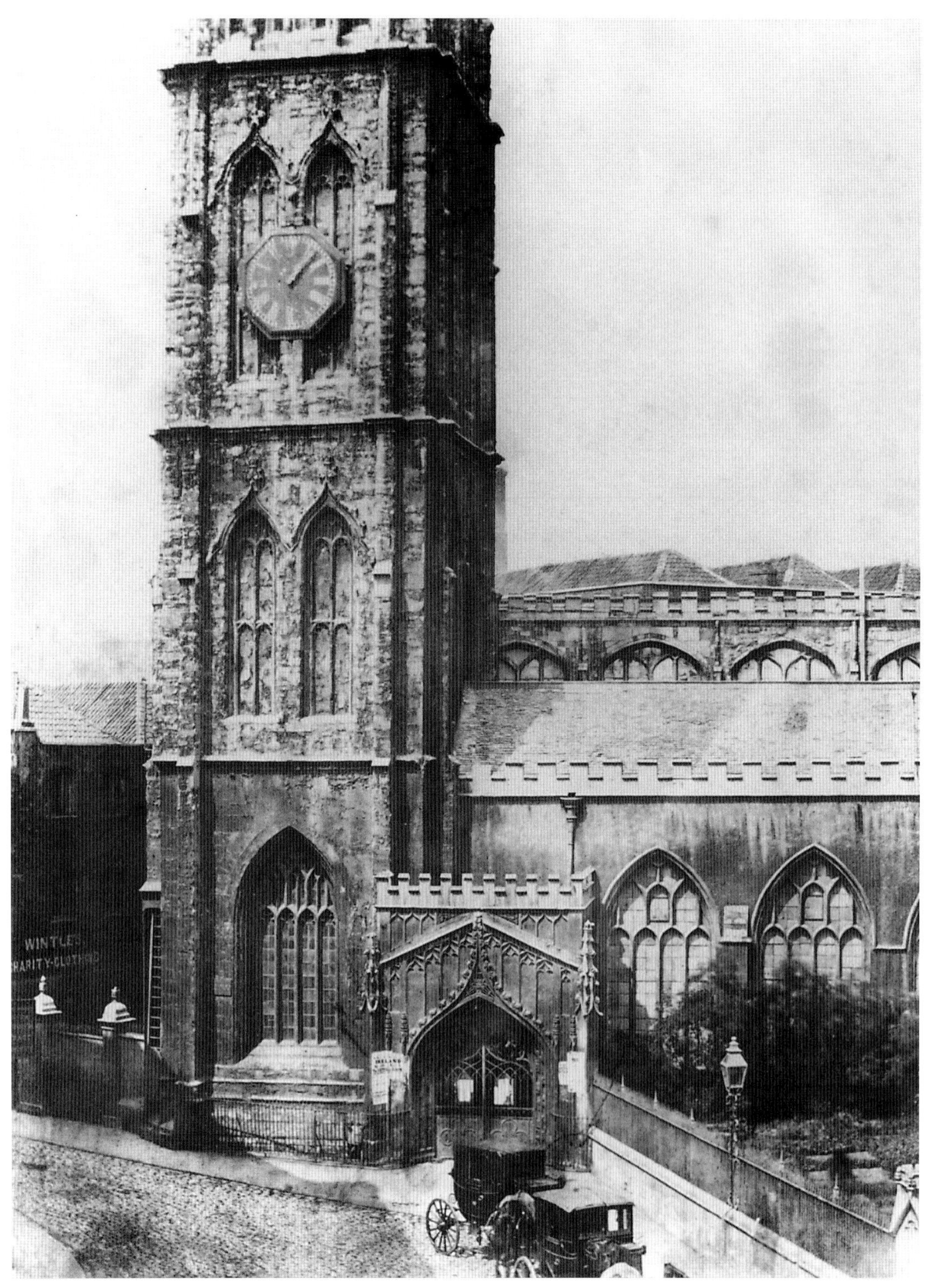

WINTLE
CHARITY-CLOTHING

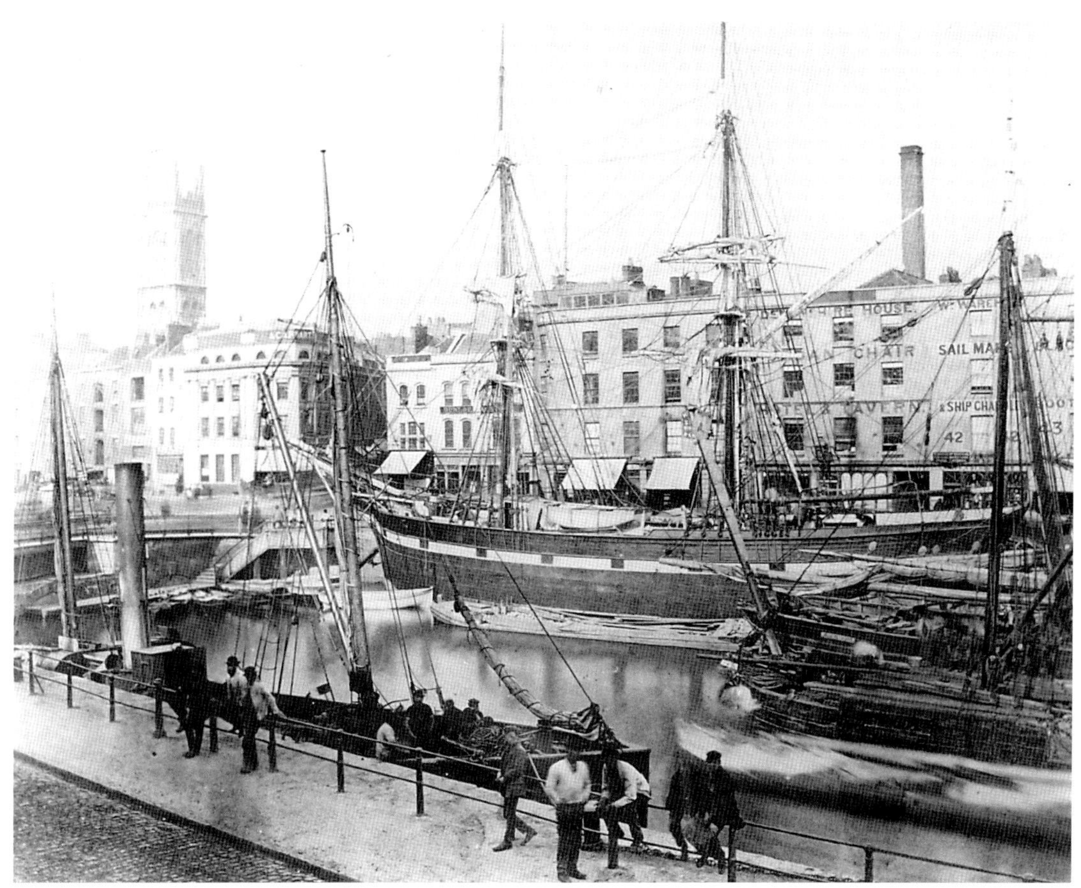

Opposite: St Stephen's Church, City and a haunting study of one of Bristol city centre's most famous towers taken in May 1858. The clock was removed when the tower was restored in the early 1860's.

Photo: Bristol Museums and Art Gallery

Above: The Sedan Chair hotel and tavern on Broad Quay. The Inn was built following the 1840 demolition of the previous Cork Tavern.

Photo: Bristol Museums and Art Gallery

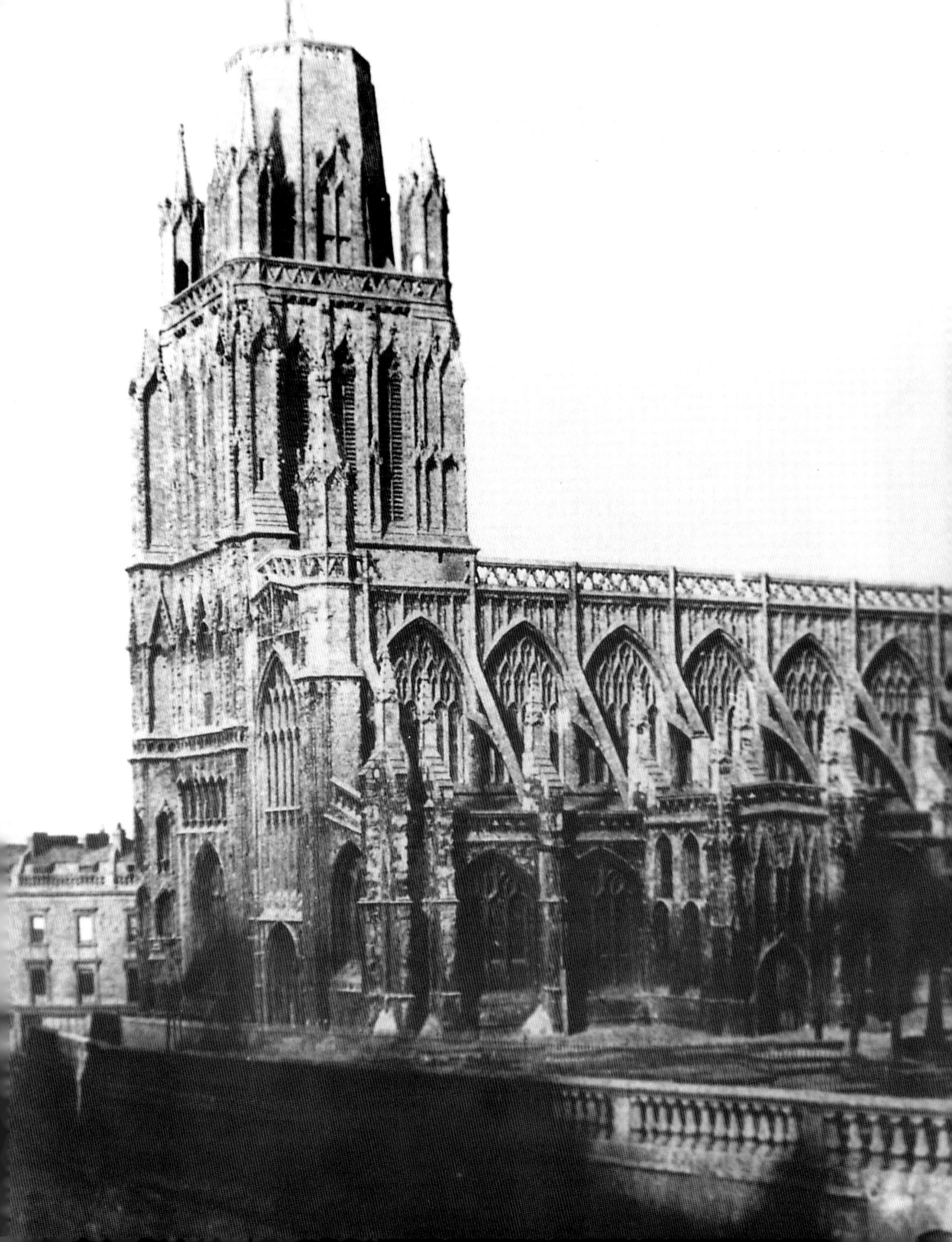

Avon Gorge with Brunel's bridge unfinished and abandoned, its piers standing like bare teeth above the cliffs. Others illustrated the haunting contrast of light and shade in deserted, narrow Bristol streets. A beautiful study of St John's Arch captured my imagination at once . . . the scene seemed so unchanged. St Mary Redcliffe, by contrast, was almost unrecognisable with its spire incomplete.

Occasionally people made an appearance. Children were caught absorbed in play. Servants and workmen were going about their daily tasks, washing clothes or standing with their road-mending tools. A family was photographed in a Redland garden in which every leaf seemed to sparkle and glitter with light. But these were not the familiar images of Victorians and Edwardians. They were neither the stiff, formal portraits of the photographic studio nor the documentary studies of crowded, busy streets. These studies had been artfully arranged and composed for the very long exposure times required in those days.

I was already very familiar with the Bristol School of Artists. I had reviewed several exhibitions of their work and written articles about them as the School became better known in the 1970s. Now I had come across a new vision of Bristol - the one seen through the lenses of photographers like Hugh Owen, his friend John Hazard and colleagues who were among the leading proponents.

There were talented, sensitive photographers working in most large British cities in the early years of photography. I cannot - much as I would like to - sustain a claim that Bristol had a School of Photographers to stand shoulder to shoulder with the Bristol School of Artists.

But the Bristol artists and early photographers through their work do offer us something very distinctive indeed - a series of identical, highly romantic subjects which inspired them in their chosen mediums. It is fascinating to see how they singled out these subjects and to see their work displayed together, both in this book and the exhibition it accompanies.

And there is another, contemporary dimension. Quite a few of these scenes are almost unchanged. Leigh Woods is instantly recognisable and so are corners of the Gorge. You have to look very closely at Hugh Owen's study of St John's

Gateway to notice that the Grand Hotel had not been built when he took his picture. We can judge how well the artists and photographers succeeded in their own right by using our own eyes and imagination if we visit the very places where they stood with their sketching pads or cameras more than a century ago.

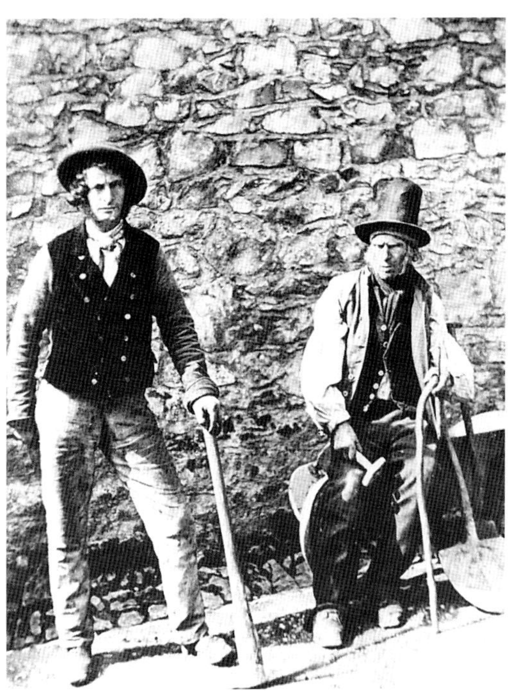

Above: Two roadmen in Redland photographed in the 1850s and one of early Bristol photography's best-known images. The standing figure perfectly expresses the Victorian belief in the dignity of labour, a theme which the great Pre-Raphaelite artist Ford Madox Brown went on to portray so forcefully in his painting Work.

Photo: Bristol Records Office

Opposite: St Mary Redcliffe Church by John Bevan Hazard (died 1892). A fine early 1850s study by Hazard using the paper negative process and a composition which enhances the elegance and symmetry of this proud building.

Photo: Bristol Records Office

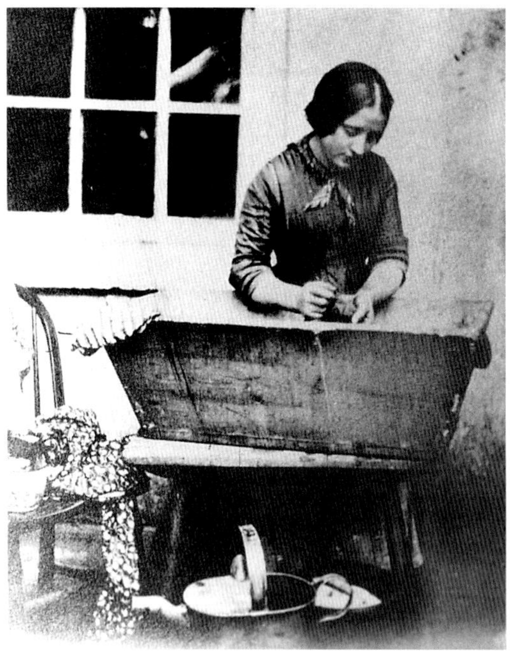

Artists had for centuries perfected the tricks of enabling their sitters to maintain difficult poses. Photographers quickly picked up these skills so that long exposures would not be ruined by inadvertant movement.

Above: A fine genre example is The Wash Tub, also from the Fedden family album. Look closely and you will see that the intent washer girl's pose is carefully arranged not only to look as unselfconcious as possible but her arms are firmly anchored for support on the edge of the tub to make her stance less cramped.

Right: Light sparkles in the garden of Redland Villa as the Fedden family hold themselves breathlessly still for this beautiful portrait. One of the treasures of their family photographic album, later presented to the City by Victor Fuller-Eberle.

Informal, natural portraiture was an exacting task for the early photographers, but it was a subject they were anxious to tackle in as artistic a way as possible.

Both photographs were taken in the 1850s.

Photo: Bristol Records Office

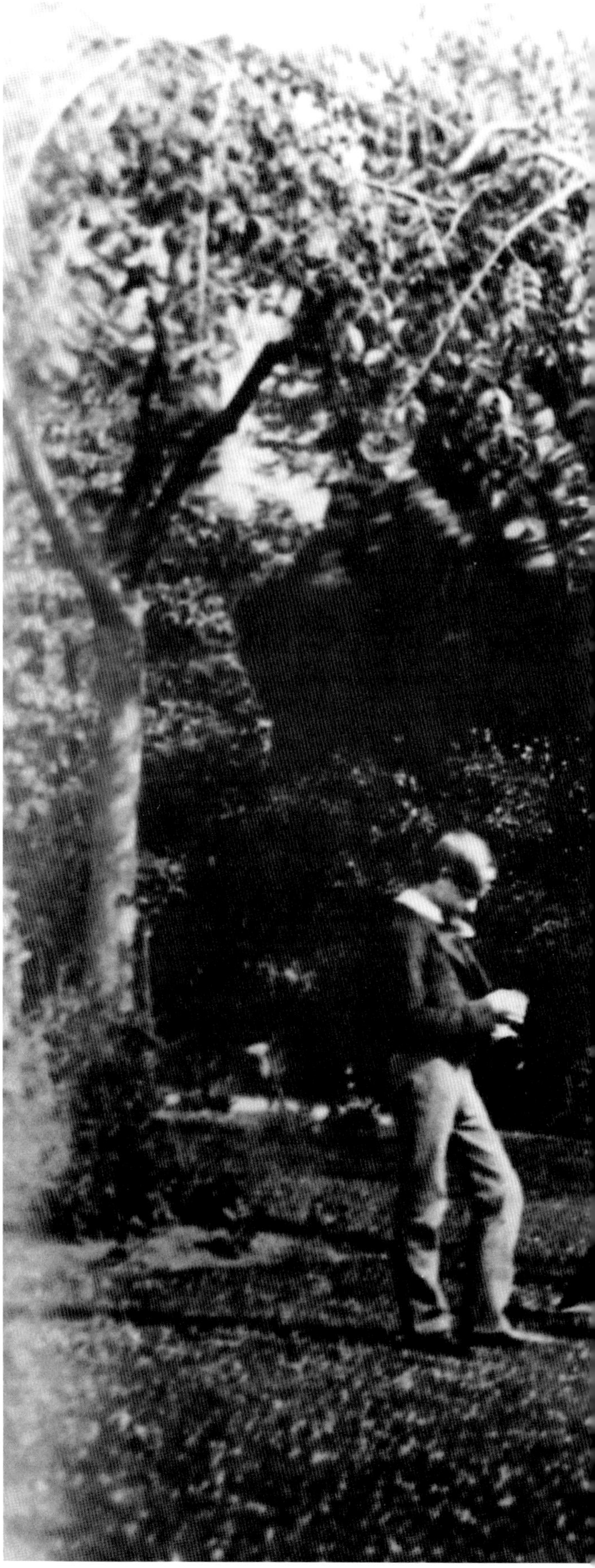

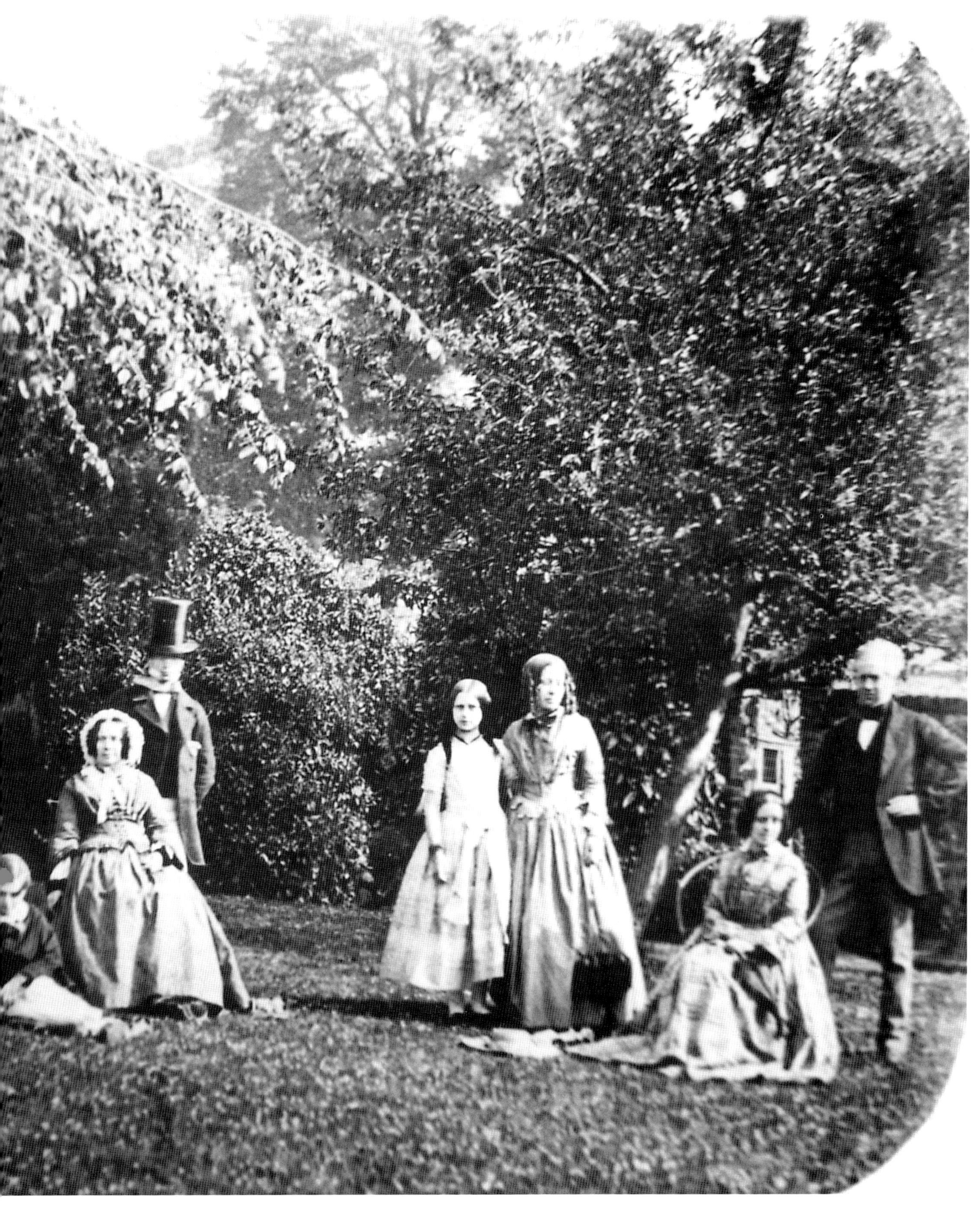

The two groups weren't strangers to each other. Some, like S.P. Jackson, combined their work as artists with their hobby as gifted amateur photographers. When Francis Danby came back to Bristol in the 1850s to stay with his friend Samuel Jackson, the latter's son S.P. Jackson took two photographs, one of Danby and his father, the other a solo portrait of Danby.

The first cameras used by Jackson and his friends were crude, bulky beasts, difficult to operate and painfully slow to record the light and the images which their lenses reflected on to sensitised surfaces. But they opened a window to a whole new world of visual detail so perfectly accurate that some artists felt their skills had been made redundant. Why spend hours sketching and painting when a camera could do the job in seconds?

As things turned out, photography had exactly the opposite effect. It offered all sorts of benefits, from sharp, close focus which confirmed an impressionist view of the world to forms of portraiture which would have been impossible in drawing or painting. The new form complemented traditional art forms and, at its best, created a new art all of its own.

These beautiful early photographs can be seen in many lights . . . as frozen moments from the past, as early compositions of photographic artistry and, seen alongside near-contemporary paintings, as object lessons in how art and photography came together. But, most of all, they should be pictures to enjoy and appreciate, just like the paintings.

The world of photography which came after Hugh Owen and the other Bristol pioneers rapidly grew more and more sophisticated as both equipment and film improved . . . and the future was to prove far more golden than even the most optimistic of the pathfinders could have dared believe.

It is no coincidence that Cartwrights, the long-established Bristol firm of solicitors, first suggested and then chose to sponsor the exhibition A Small Light In The Far West.

Cartwrights, Bristol and the dawn of photography have close historic links. The firm of Danger and Cartwright, as it was originally known, was founded in 1836 in Corn Street in the heart of the city's commercial district. Its foundation lies midway between the greatest triumphs of the Bristol School of Artists in the early 19th century and Bristol photography's golden age in the mid-1800s. Cartwrights saw the exhibition as an opportunity to celebrate both the history and the pioneering spirit of a forward-looking city which was as prepared then to explore the latest technology as it is now.

The exhibition coincides with the year of the Festival of the Sea and preparations for the many events to be staged celebrating the 500th anniversary of John Cabot's voyage across the Atlantic as the first modern European to make a fully recorded landfall on mainland America. It is a time when the eyes of the world will be on Bristol . . . and perhaps a recognition of Bristol's place in the story of photography will be one of the benefits.

Every now and again, that adventurous spirit and the excitement of the early photographers was recaptured. This book ends as it began, with a photographer trumpeting the very latest technological wonder of the day. Fox Talbot chose the SS Great Britain. Our unknown photographer was up on the Downs to capture the Edwardians' wonder at the novelty of flying as two women watch Maurice Tetard take off in a Bristol Boxkite.

It is a thrilling picture worthy of Hugh Owen himself.

Opposite: The Shakespeare Inn on Victoria Street with the tilting tower of Temple Church in the background photographed on a bright, sunny day. This delightful group of period buildings was typical of an old Bristol which charmed artists and photographers alike.

Photo: Bristol Museums & Art Gallery

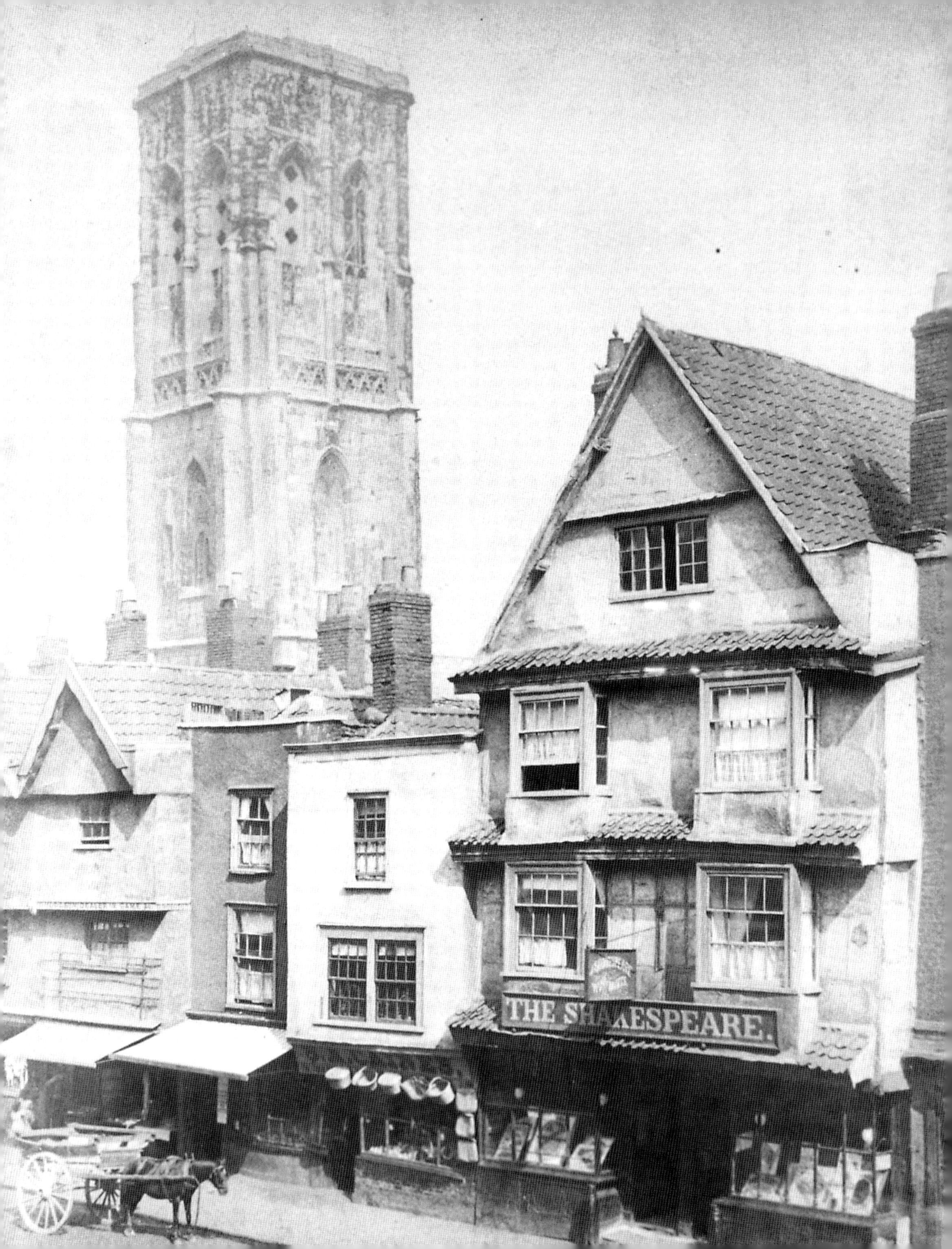
THE SHAKESPEARE.

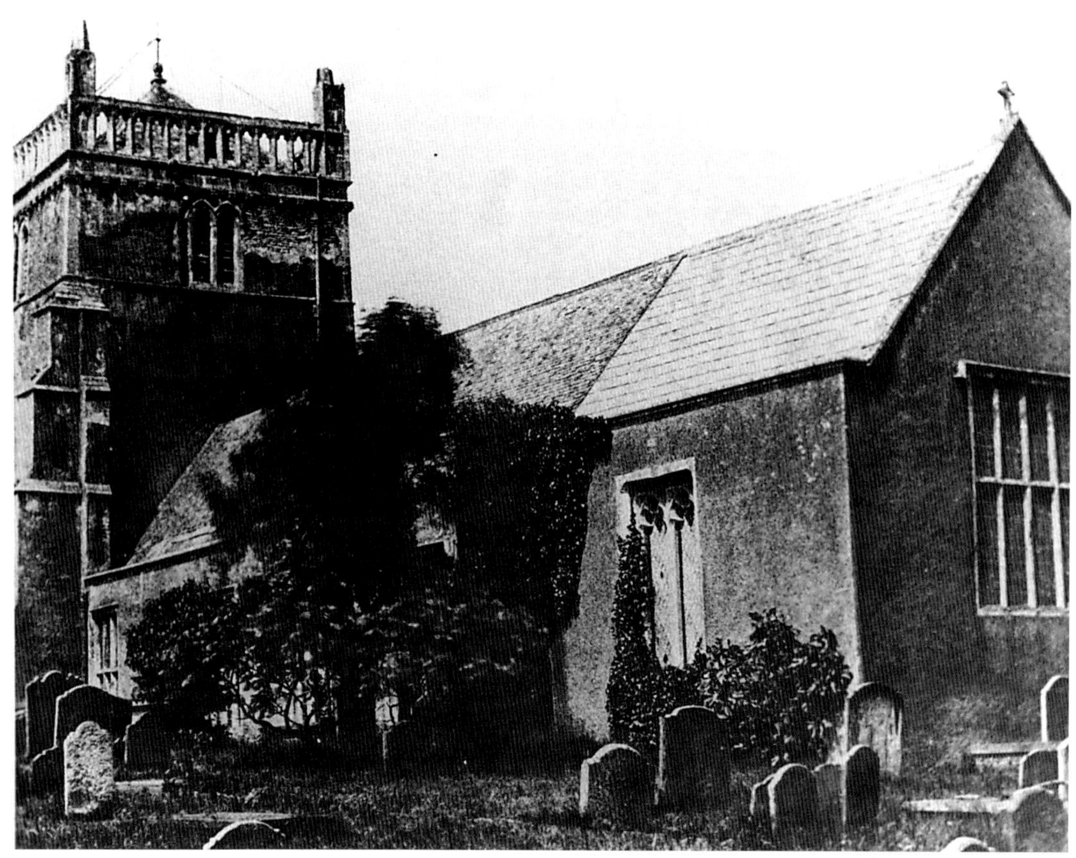

Above: Bedminster Old Church before 1855. Early photographers were quick to realise the value of photographs as documentary records. Several important Bristol buildings due for demolition or alteration were photographed for posterity. This is Bedminster Old Church before it was rebuilt in the 1850s. The church was wrecked in the Bristol blitzes and the rubble finally cleared away in 1967.

Photo: Bristol Records Office

Opposite: St John's Gateway by Hugh Owen (1808-1897). This masterly Calotype was taken in the early 1850s. By now Owen had become supremely confident, using shadow, light and careful composition to create a hauntingly evocative study which is widely regarded as one of early photography's masterpieces.

Photo: Bristol Records Office

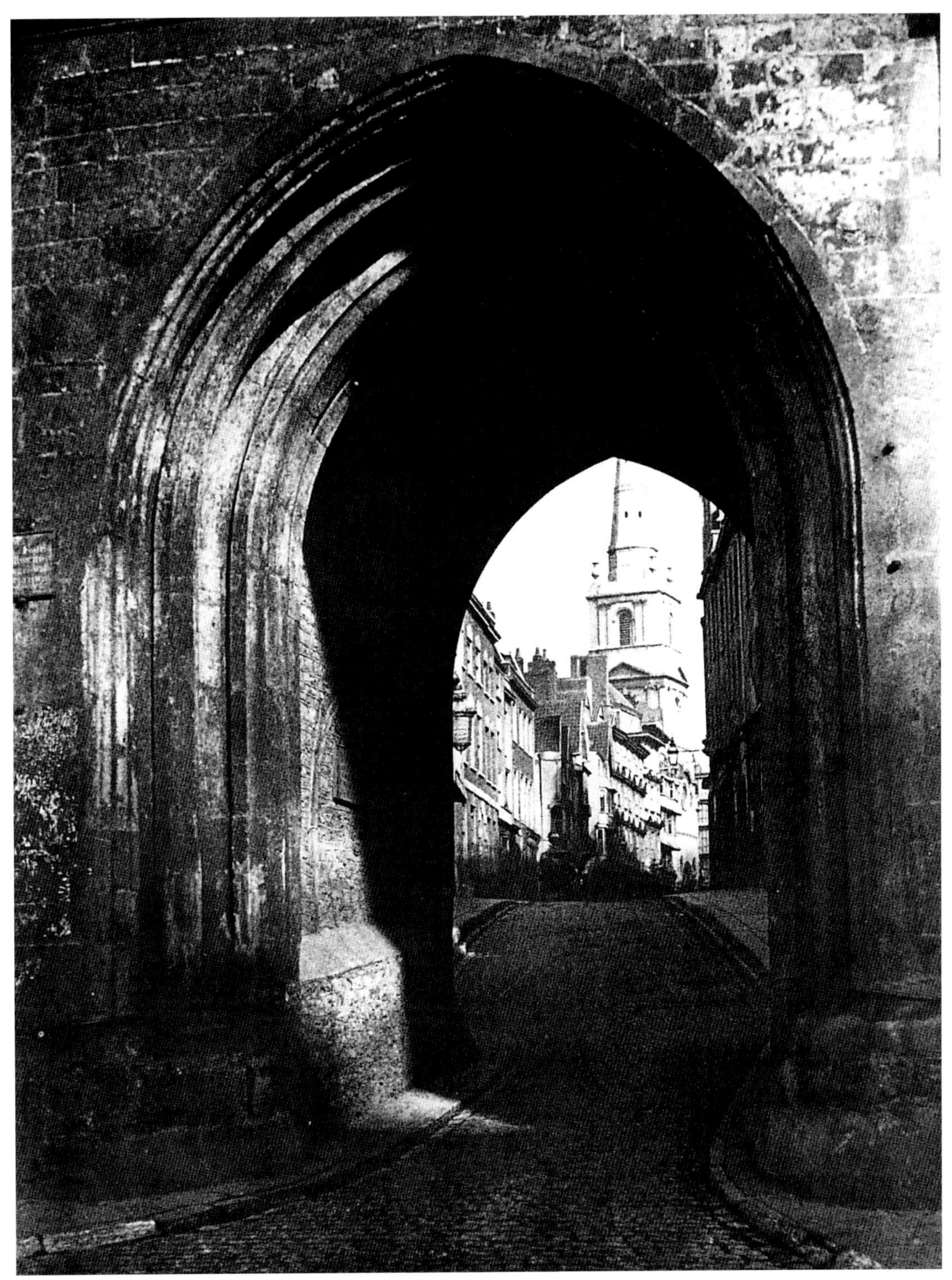

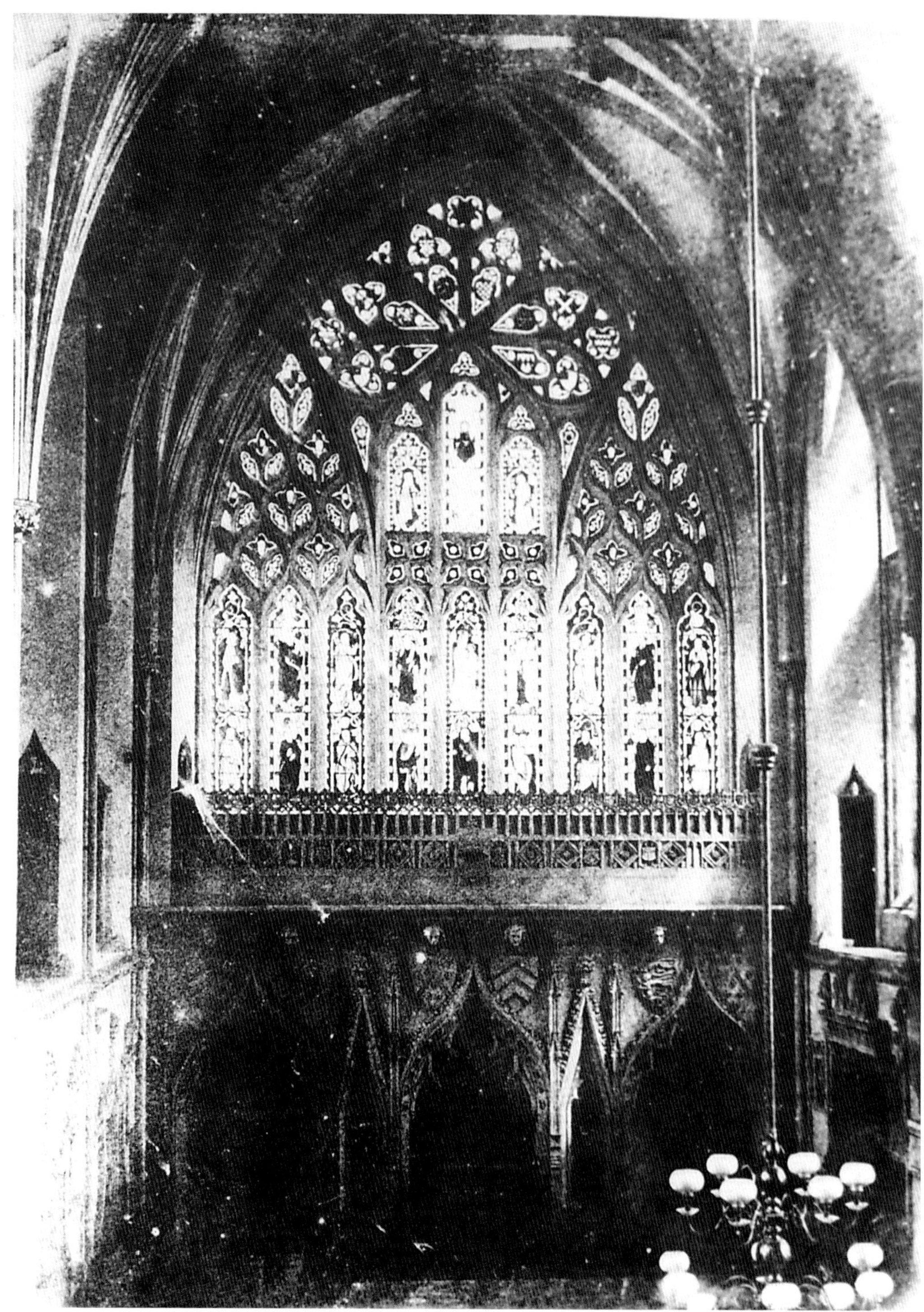

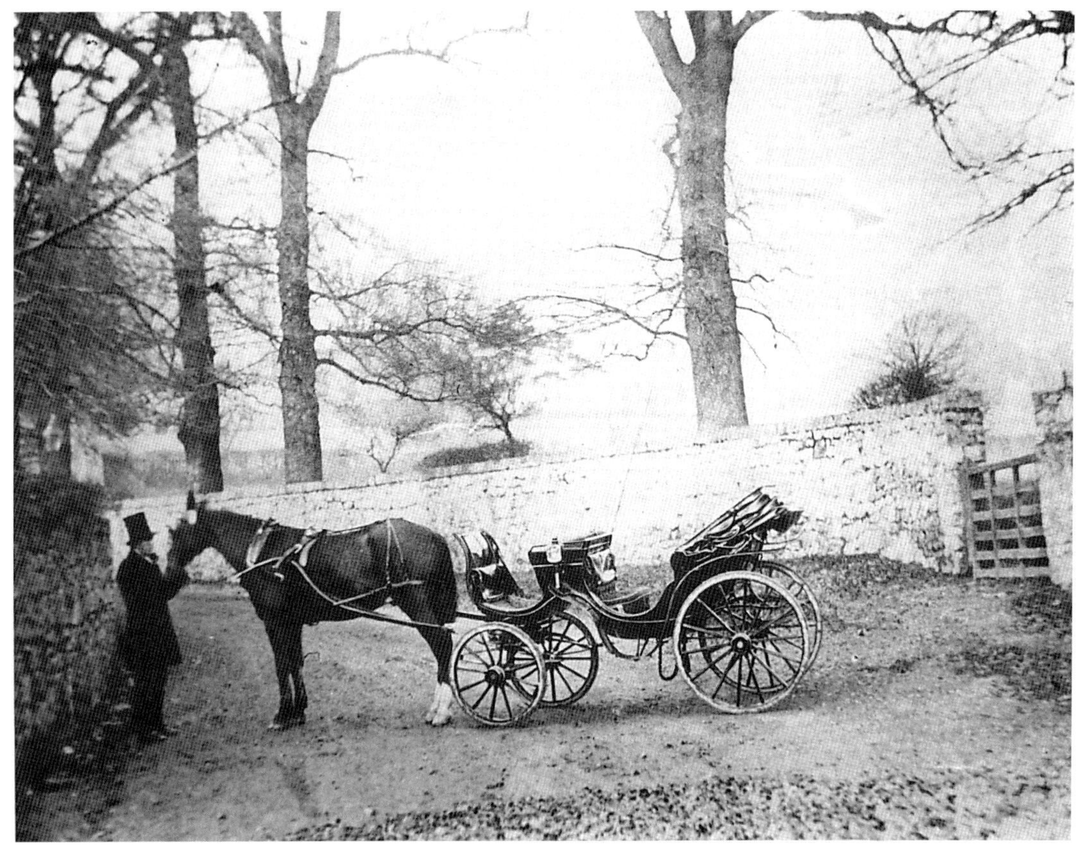

Above: Redland, then a peaceful outpost of Bristol. A one-horse carriage is carefully positioned in what is believed be today's Elm Lane area. The leafy, near-rural Redland area provided several popular subjects for the first photographers.

Photo: Bristol Records Office

Opposite: Bristol Cathedral's Eastern Lady Chapel photographed in the 1850s. To the Victorian eye, one of photography's most astonishing achievements was the mass of detail it offered. The great art critic/artist John Ruskin summed up this achievement thus: "Anyone who has worked, blundered and stammered as I have for four days and then sees the thing he has been trying to do so long in vain, done perfectly and faultlessly in half a minute, won't abuse it (photography) afterwards".

Photo: Bristol Records Office

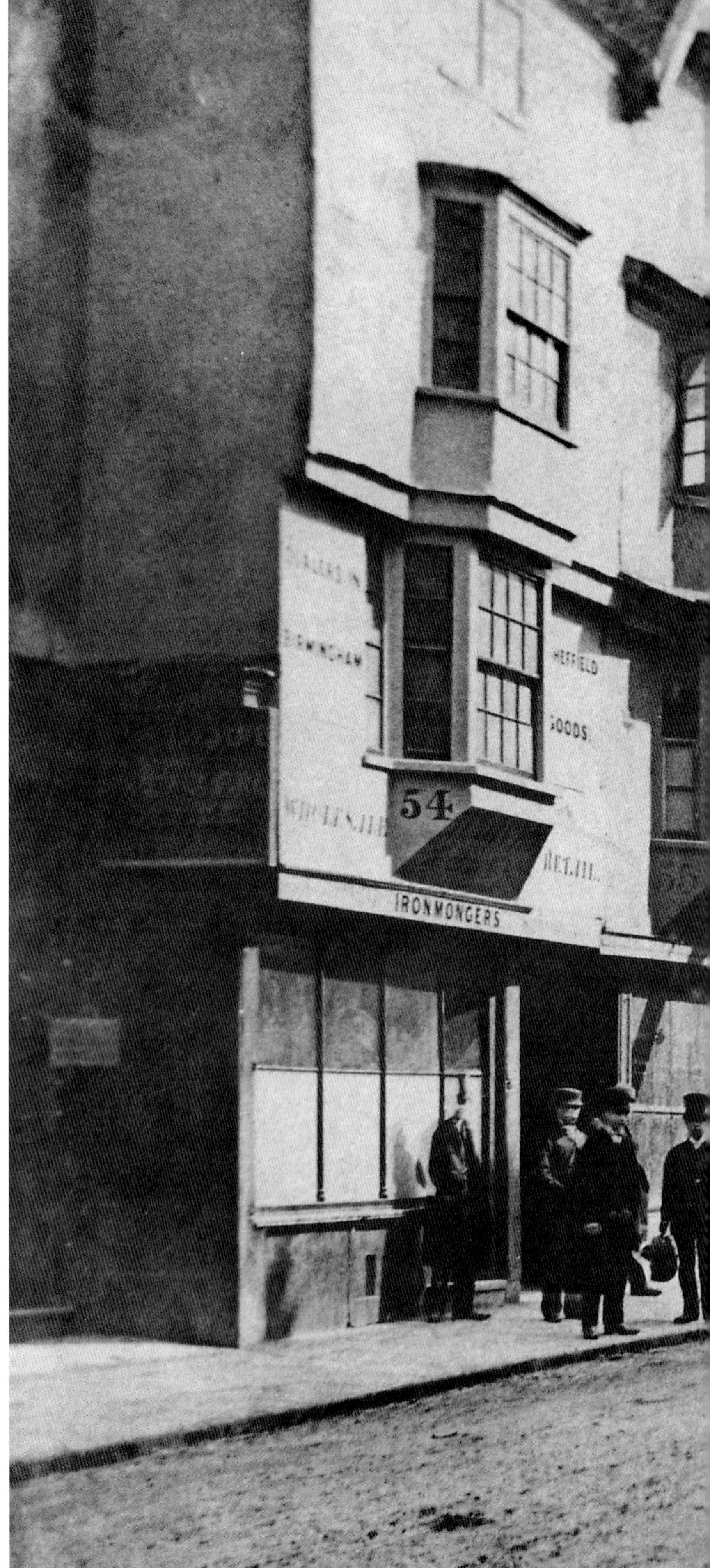

Bright sunlight pinpoints every detail of the soon-to-be-demolished facades in Broad Street in this arresting study looking up towards Christ Church – the Grand Hotel stands here today. The top-hatted bystanders freeze their poses obligingly, excited by the novelty of a large-scale group photograph.

Photo: Bristol Museums and Art Gallery

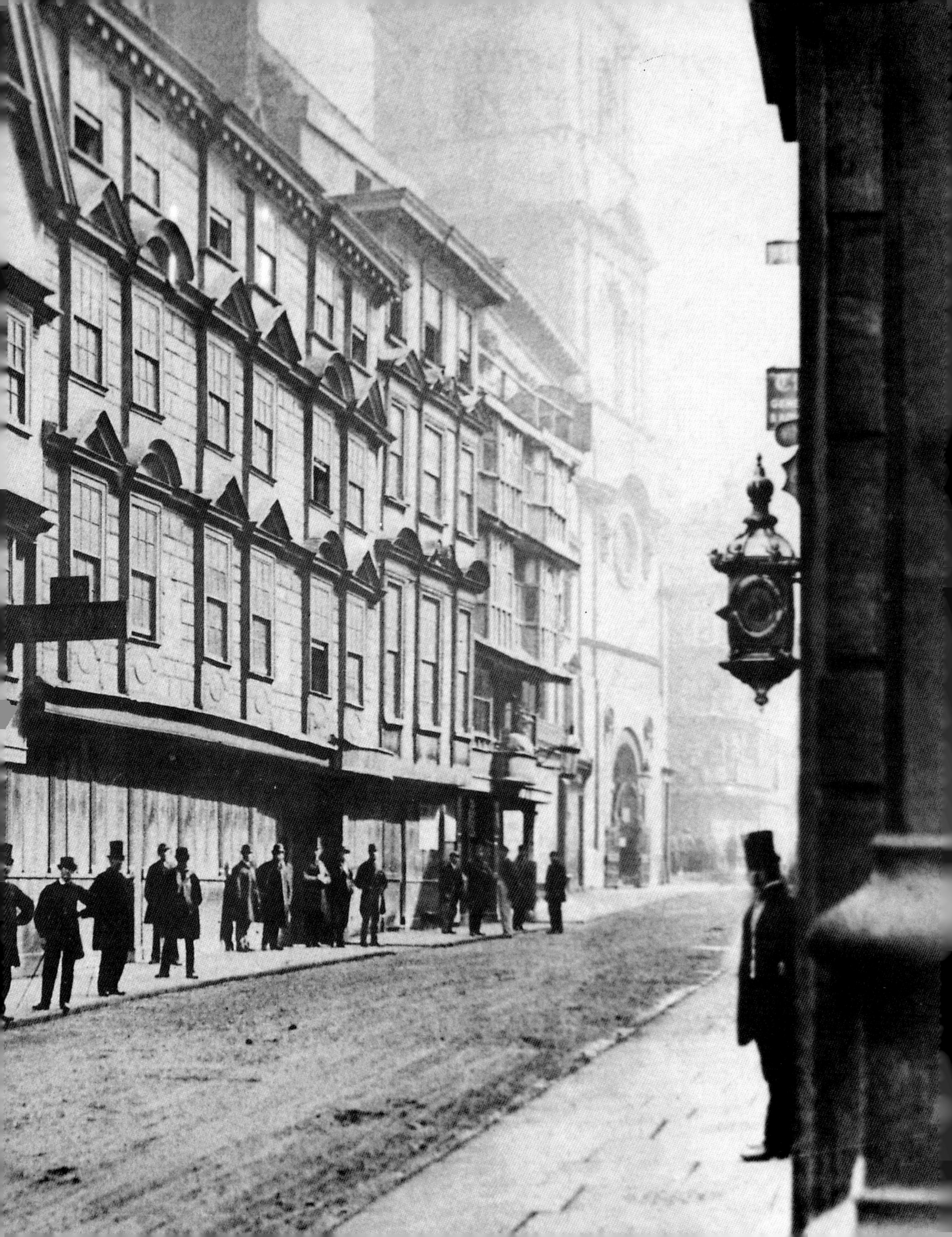

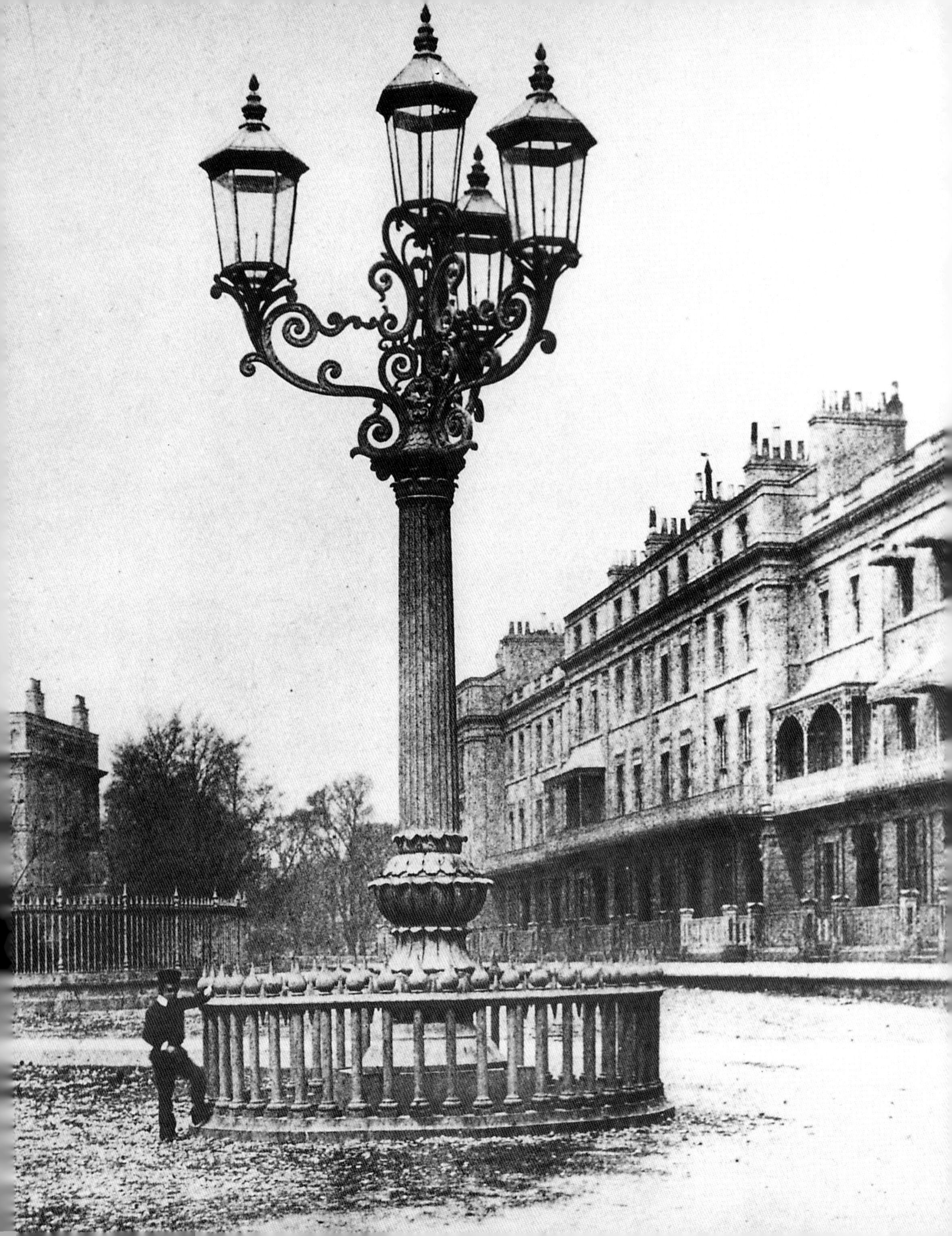

City of Change

To get the most out of these early photographs of Bristol, it is a great help to know something about the city at the time most of the pictures were taken and why it looked the way it did in the mid-1800s.

By 1850 Bristol should have been able to boast one of the most spectacular entrances to any harbour in the world. The dream was of a procession of ships from every corner of the globe sailing up and down the River Avon bounded by romantic cliffsides and, spanning the skyline above the deep-cut gorge, a breathtaking suspension bridge decorated in the Ancient Egyptian style.

The reality was two abandoned piles of masonry glaring at each other across an Avon which was hardly bustling with trade. At low tide, with the river's steep mudbanks revealed, the place looked a sludgy, glutinous mess.

Photography was just one of the many revolutionary new-fangled technologies which were transforming the lives of the Victorians and challenging long-established citadels like Bristol. The industrial revolution was up and running - there was no room for complacency in an increasingly competitive Britain.

By 1850 Bristol had barely managed to clear up the debris, physical, financial, political and social, of the dreadful Reform Riots of 19 years earlier when a drunken mob had taken over the streets for several days and nights while the authorities cowered on the sidelines. It took a lethal charge by armed cavalry through the riot's centre in Queen Square to restore order. But by then the damage had been done and Bristol's already rocky reputation suffered a blow from which it took years to recover.

Bristol had lost faith in itself. It had believed that the glory days of the 17th and 18th centuries would go on forever. That had been the age when it found itself perfectly placed to exploit the triangular slaving and trading route from Britain to Africa, the New World and back and the growing, direct transatlantic trade to the Colonies and America. The city's wealth was reflected in magnificent public buildings like the Corn Exchange, grand merchants' town houses and, later, the smart crescents, squares and terraces of the new suburb of Clifton.

The cornerstone of this success was the ancient port of Bristol. But by the end of the 18th century

Opposite: Victoria Square, Clifton, in the 1850s, a bold photograph with a vivid sense of scale, particularly in the placing of the little boy who is dwarfed by the dominant great four-lantern street light and facade of the terraced houses behind.

Photo: Bristol Records Office

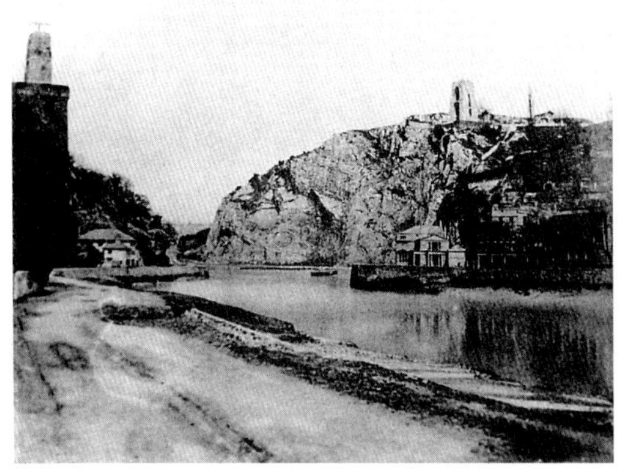

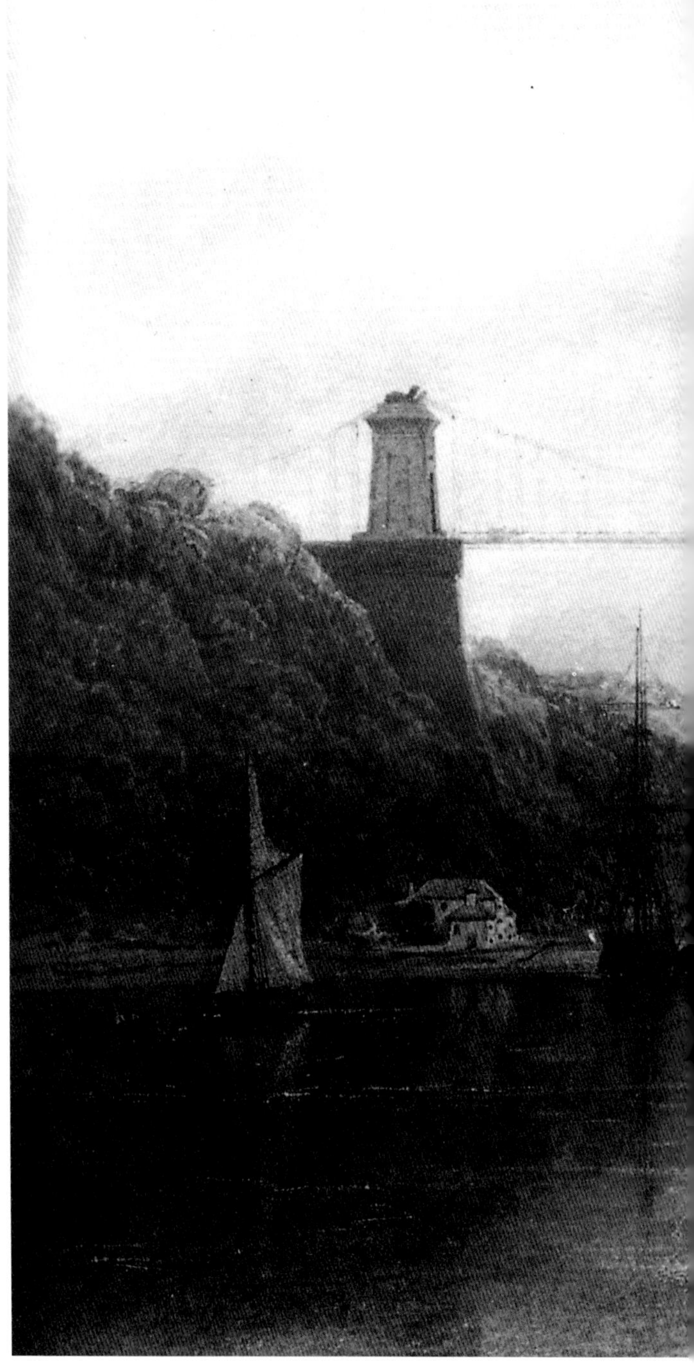

Above and right: The Clifton Suspension Bridge as it should have looked… and the 1850s reality.

The Proposed Suspension Bridge from Rownham Ferry by Samuel Jackson (1794-1869) shows an idyllic Avon Gorge crowned by the original Egyptian-style design for the Clifton Suspension Bridge by Isambard Kingdom Brunel (1806-1859). His designs were later modified after work halted in the aftermath of the dreadful Bristol Riots of October 1831.

To the first photographers, the sight of Brunel's two gaunt piers glaring at each other across the gorge was a symbol of Bristol's decline… and a potent image to be captured for posterity.

Watercolour: Bristol Museums and Art Gallery

Photo: Bristol Records Office

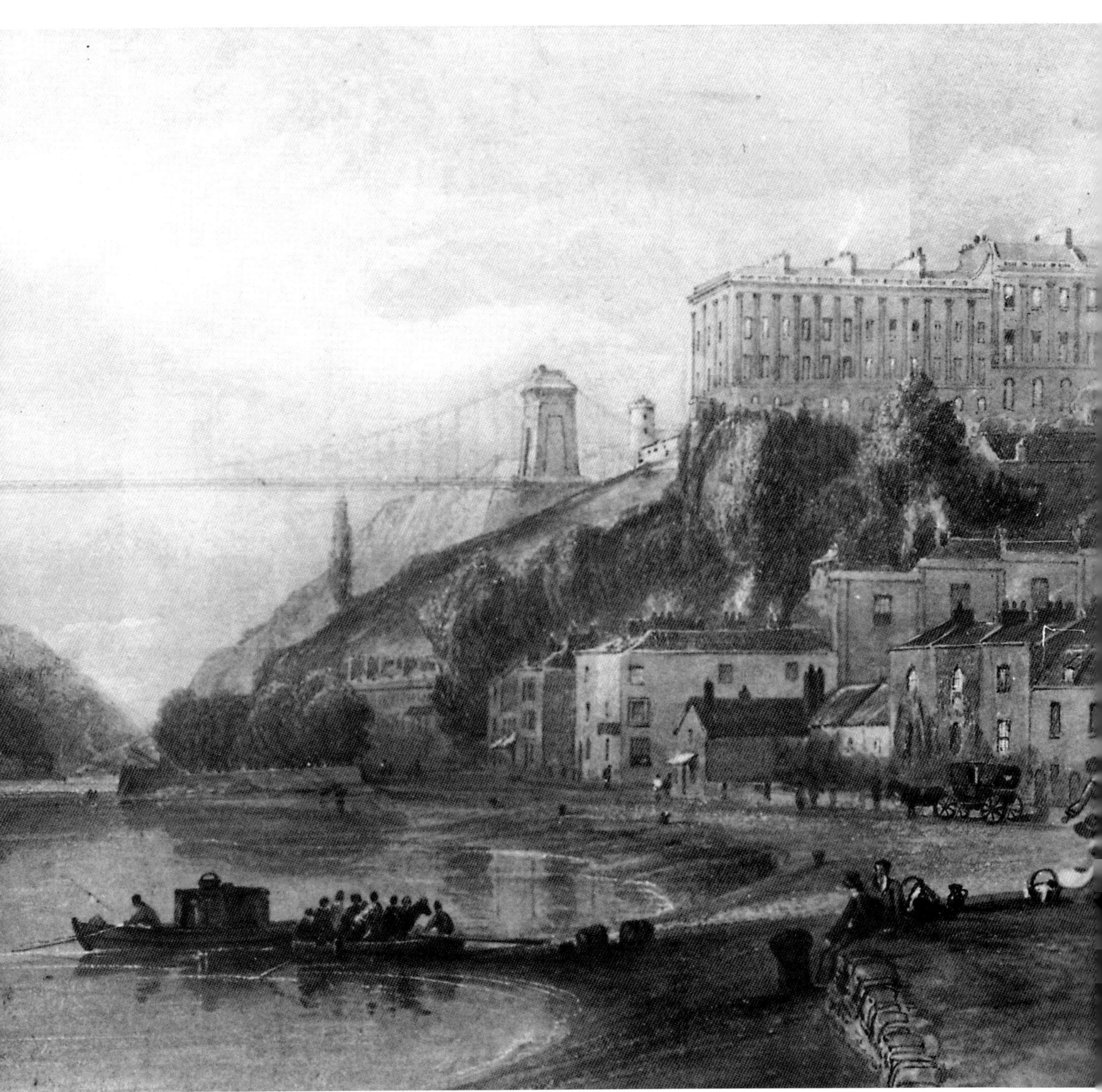

the by now archaic, overpriced harbour which could only be approached along a winding river with dangerously high tides and lethal mudbanks looked less attractive to canny merchantmen. They sought out safer, cheaper ports like Liverpool.

That grim sailors' joke "Shipshape And Bristol Fashion", a warning that weaker boats would break their backs rising and falling on the banks of the tidal harbour, had become infamous. Work on a non-tidal "Floating Harbour" in the early 1800s came too little, too late. Bristol had lost its place as one of the world's leading ports.

The civil unrest of the Bristol Riots was, on the surface, a violent demonstration for Parliamentary Reform. The deeper cause was an almost universal loathing for the city's smug, reactionary, self-electing leaders who were blamed - quite fairly, in most cases - for the financial problems it was facing.

The newly-emerging middle classes, who would go on to rescue the city's fortunes, not only stood on the sidelines in Queen Square when the mob began to riot, but some even encouraged the rioters. One of the upwardly mobile observers who did lend a hand was the young engineer Isambard Kingdom Brunel, who joined friends in saving civic furniture from the blazing Mansion House.

The 23-year-old Brunel had been attracted to Bristol for the same aesthetic reasons that painters and early photographers had been drawn to its landscape.

He had been badly injured in a frightening accident when his father Marc Brunel's tunnel under the Thames had suffered a partial collapse as a huge wave of water crashed in. Isambard Kingdom wanted somewhere pleasant to recuperate and he chose Clifton. It had a lively social scene, plenty of attractive young women and, on its doorstep, the precipitous allure of the Avon Gorge, secluded Leigh Woods and the expansive Downs. It was a perfect place for the ambitious young civil engineer to convalesce.

So he was very excited when a competition to span the Avon Gorge was announced and his proposed entry won. It was a masterpiece of design – a beautifully proportioned suspension bridge with Ancient Egyptian motifs including sphinxes and a vulture's open wings.

A ceremonial start was made in 1830.

Sadly, it wasn't just buildings which went up in flames during the following year's riots. Brunel's thrilling vision of one of the wonders of the world was a major casualty. He never saw his beloved bridge completed. The riots halted the work for five years and even though building was resumed, the money quickly ran out yet again because of the shaky state of the local economy.

Every time Brunel glanced along the Avon or walked across the Downs or through Leigh Woods, the sight of his unfinished bridge must have unutterably depressed even his optimistic spirits.

Instead of proclaiming Bristol's wealth and importance, his bridge - or what there was of it - was left a ruin, a symbol of the decline into a provincial backwater. It was a haunting monument for the early photographers, who knew a telling sight when they saw one.

This failure clearly spurred Brunel on to other endeavours and he tirelessly went on to do his best to drag Bristol into the 19th century. He improved the docks and built two wonderful ships, the Great Western, launched in 1837 and the SS Great Britain, launched by Prince Albert in 1843. He widened the city's horizons with his Great Western Railway, providing a swift, efficient, reliable link with London.

But that was just part of a much grander scheme. He wanted to make Bristol the Gateway To America and Europe's busiest transatlantic

Opposite: The close proximity of the ancient harbour at the heart of mercantile Bristol provided early photographers with many wonderful opportunities to try out their cameras and equipment on substantial subjects such as this wooden, three-masted barque undergoing repair in a dry-dock located at the south end of St Augustine's Reach in Deans Marsh.

Again, the camera readily captures details that even the most meticulous and technically competent marine artists such as Nicholas Pocock (1740-1821) or Joseph Walter (1783-1856) perforce had to omit for the sake of style or clarity.

Photo: Bristol Museums and Art Gallery

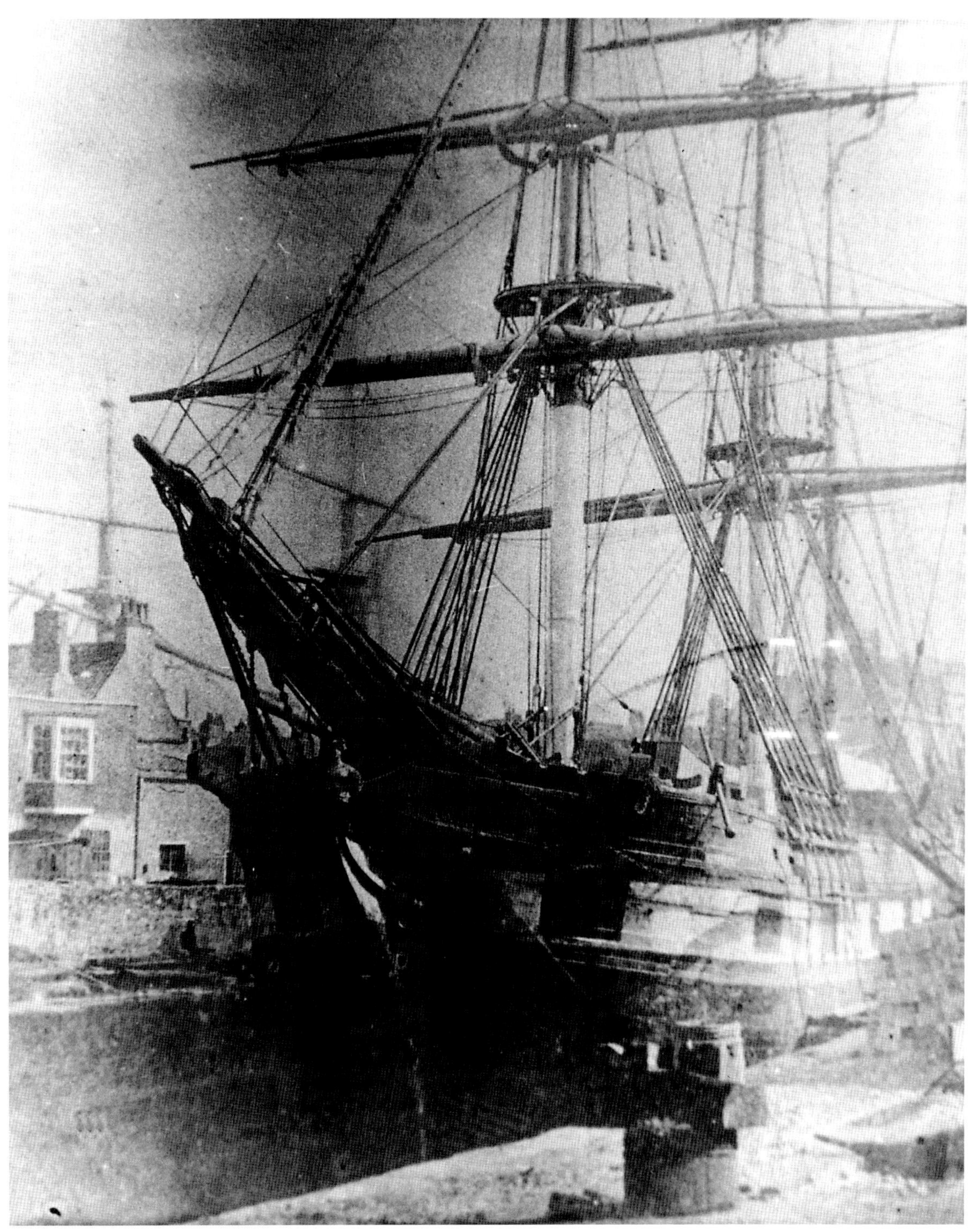

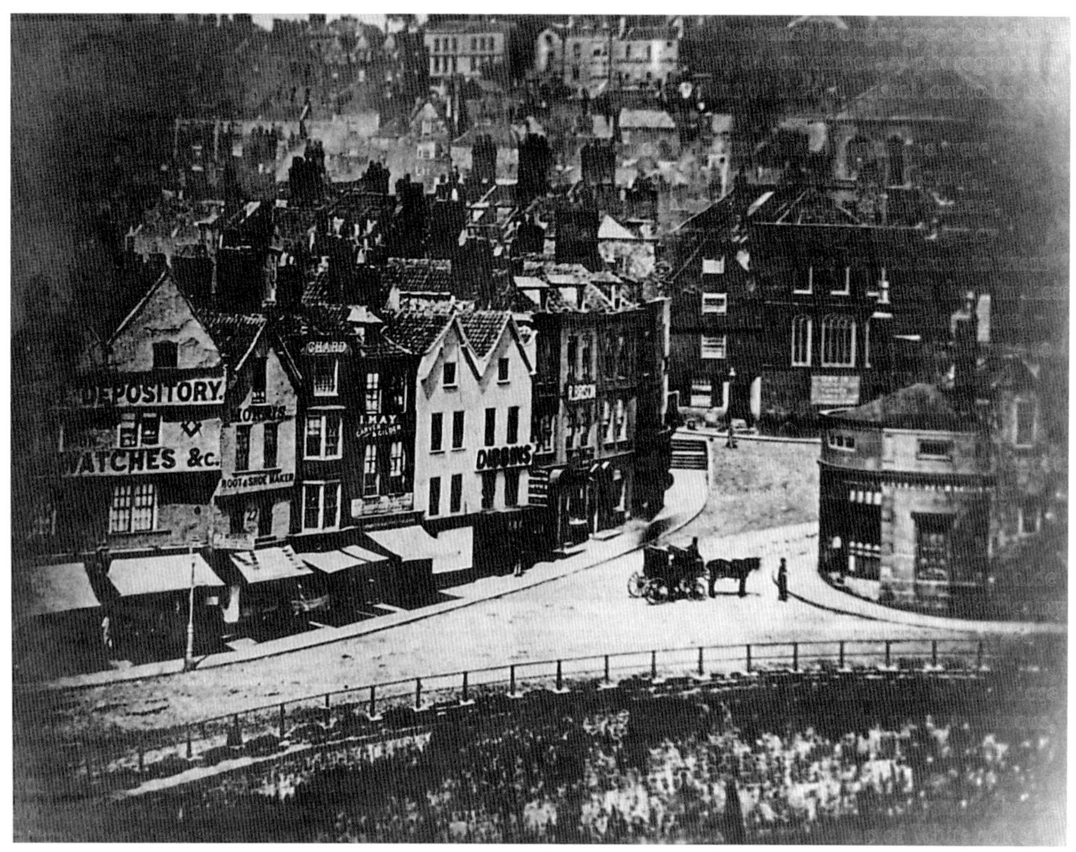

Above: The early photographer, picturing St Augustine's Back from across the city centre, relies on a horse and carriage to provide his foreground interest.

Opposite: St Augustine's Parade c 1825 by Samuel Jackson (1794-1869), a fine scene of a busy, thriving Bristol. The group of men relaying cobbles in the foreground is taken directly from W.H. Pyne's Microcosm, a book published in 1806 with the specific purpose of providing landscape painters with suitable foreground groups of figures

Watercolour and Photo: Bristol Museums and Art Gallery

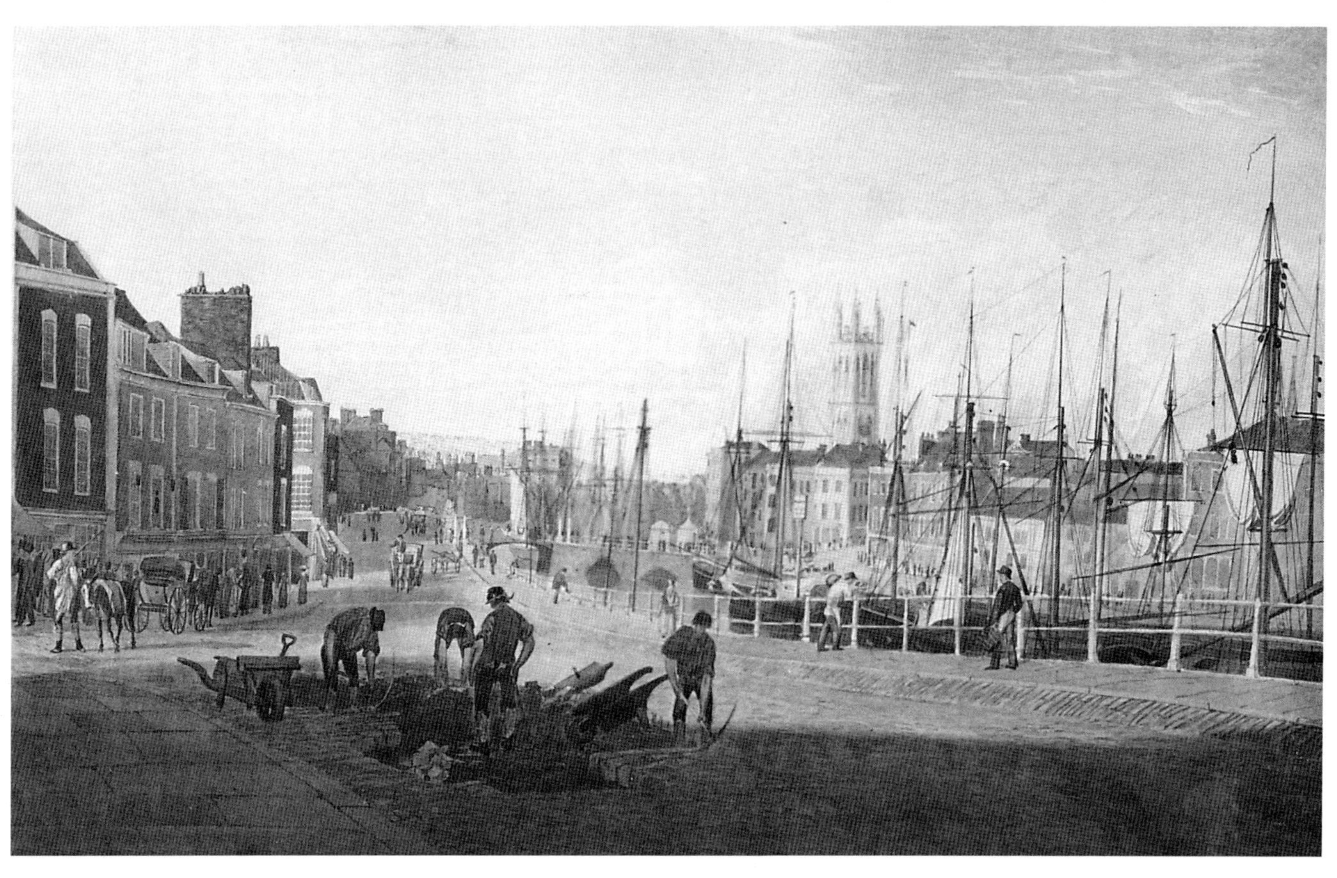

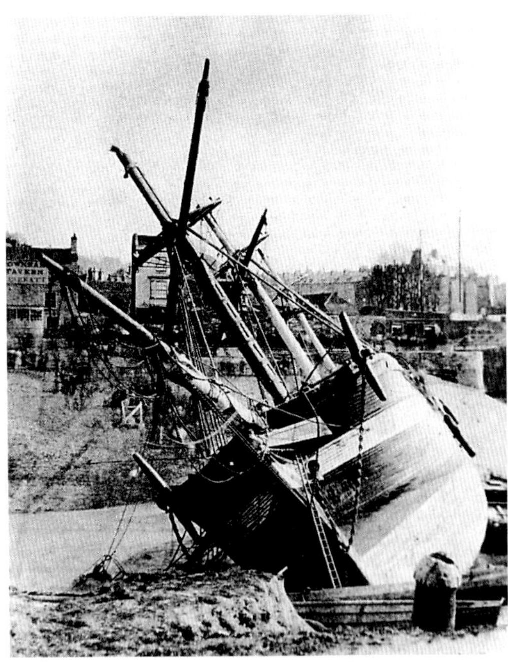

Above: The Refuge Stranded by John Bevan Hazard (died 1892). Hazard lived in Dowry Square, Hotwells, a very short walk from the Cumberland Basin, so news of the stranding of a ship only a few hundred yards away must have reached him quickly on March 13 1854. He was soon on the scene with his camera. His photograph shows the Liverpool ship the Refuge stranded on treacherous mudbanks just downstream of Cumberland Basin after she ran into the Somerset bank of the River Avon. The head-on angle is particularly effective.

Photo: Bristol Records Office

Opposite: The fanciful Black Rock Pumping Station in the Avon Gorge, a favourite subject for early photographers. It was commissioned by the Society of Merchant Venturers and designed by Isambard Kingdom Brunel (1806-1859) to pump water from a large spring up to the growing suburb of Clifton.

Photo: Bristol Museums & Art Gallery

passenger port. His dream went thus: Transatlantic travellers would be whisked down from London to Bristol on his railway where they would spend a restful night or two at his splendid hotel behind College Green - the former hotel has been renamed Brunel House and is now the headquarters of Bristol City Council's planning department - before boarding his latest ocean liner for a comfortable crossing to New York.

Brunel's dream of seamless travel never materialised as it proved a devil of a job to squeeze the SS Great Britain liner out of the narrow City Docks and she sailed away down the Avon, never to be seen again by Victorian Bristol.

If Brunel had had his way, we would have inherited albums of early photographs of a cosmopolitan Avon adorned with smart new ocean liners. Instead the most striking legacy left by Fox Talbot's fellow photographers show an earlier generation of sailing boats, wrecks and strandings on the tidal waterway.

One of early Victorian photography's most dramatic achievements is that arresting 1858 series of documentary pictures of the top-hatted, cigar-chewing Brunel as the ultimate Man of Iron. He is seen fretting and fuming at the heart-stopping launch of his monster the Great Eastern on the Thames at London and posed against the dramatic backdrop of huge chains. It would have been wonderful to link photography and Brunel directly together in Bristol but I have not, sadly, found a trace or a mention of a photograph of him in his adoptive city.

Ironically, he must have known Hugh Owen, who worked as Chief Cashier to the Great Western Railway and lived for a time in part of the original Temple Meads building designed by Brunel and used as his drawing rooms during the epic construction of the railway.

Owen and his friends obviously admired Brunel's design skills and one of their favourite subjects was the charming Italianate and then new Black Rock Pumping station in the Avon Gorge which Brunel built in 1845 to tap clean springwater and pump it up to the gentrified heights of Clifton.

Although the inspired Brunel did his best for Bristol, the city was slow to seize the many opportunities offered by new technology and the dynamic spirit of the young Victorian age.

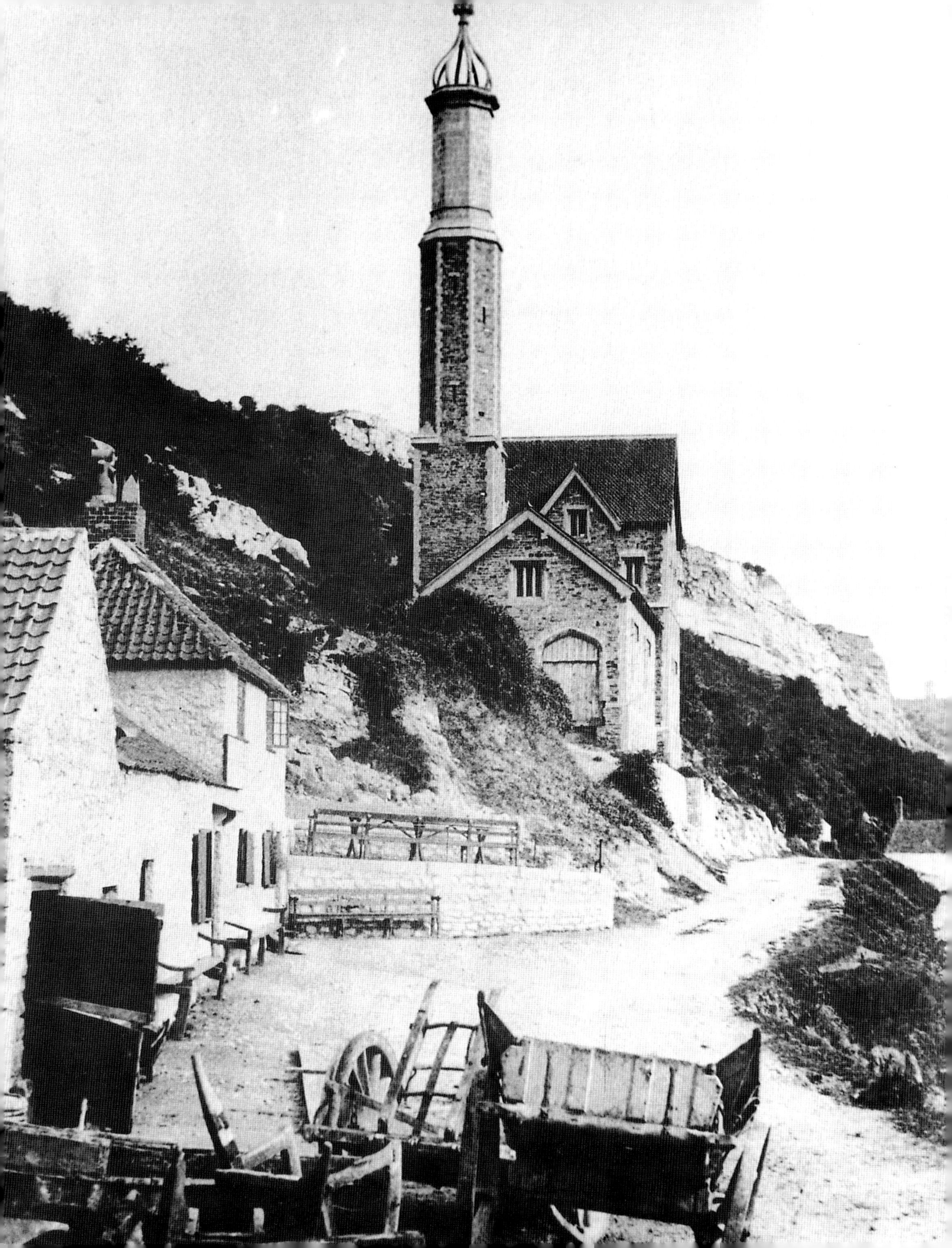

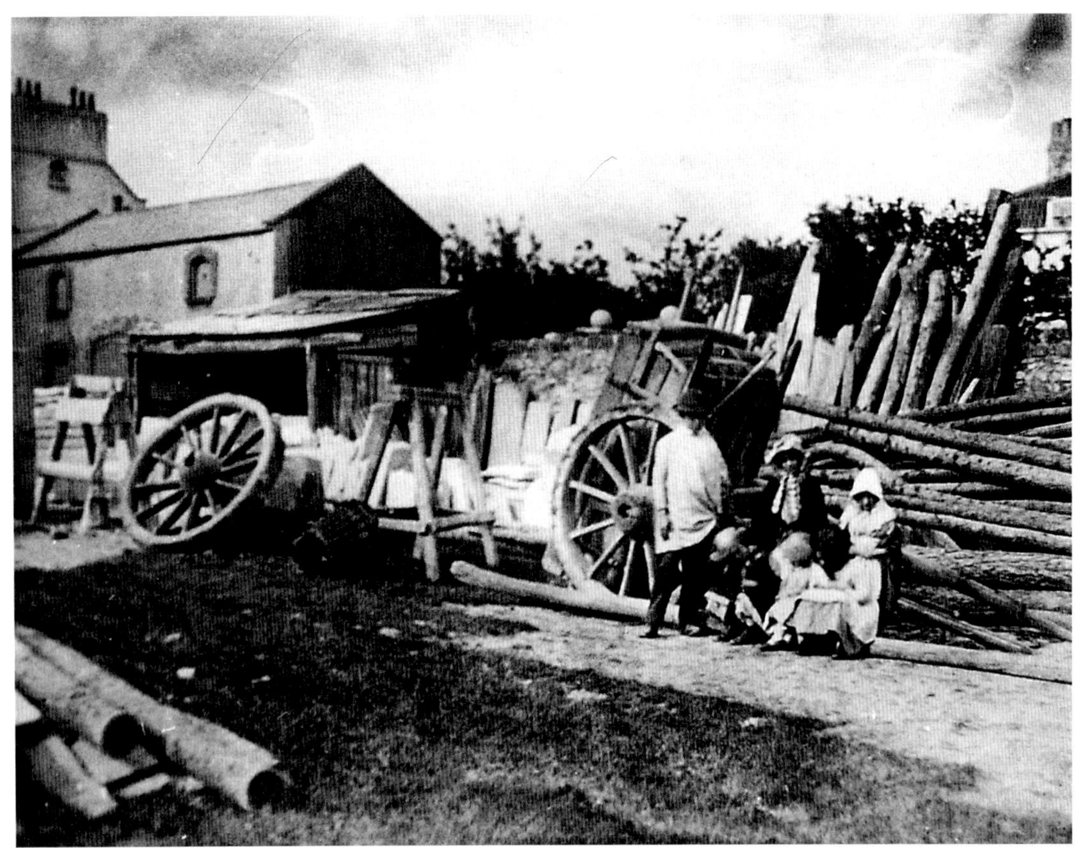

The timber yard in Hampton Road, Redland,
photographed from Woodland Terrace in 1854.
Though the scene is much altered today two of the
buildings, one on the extreme left (today's 130
Hampton Road) and the other on the far right (today's
6 Leyton Villas) still survive.

Photo: Bristol Records Office

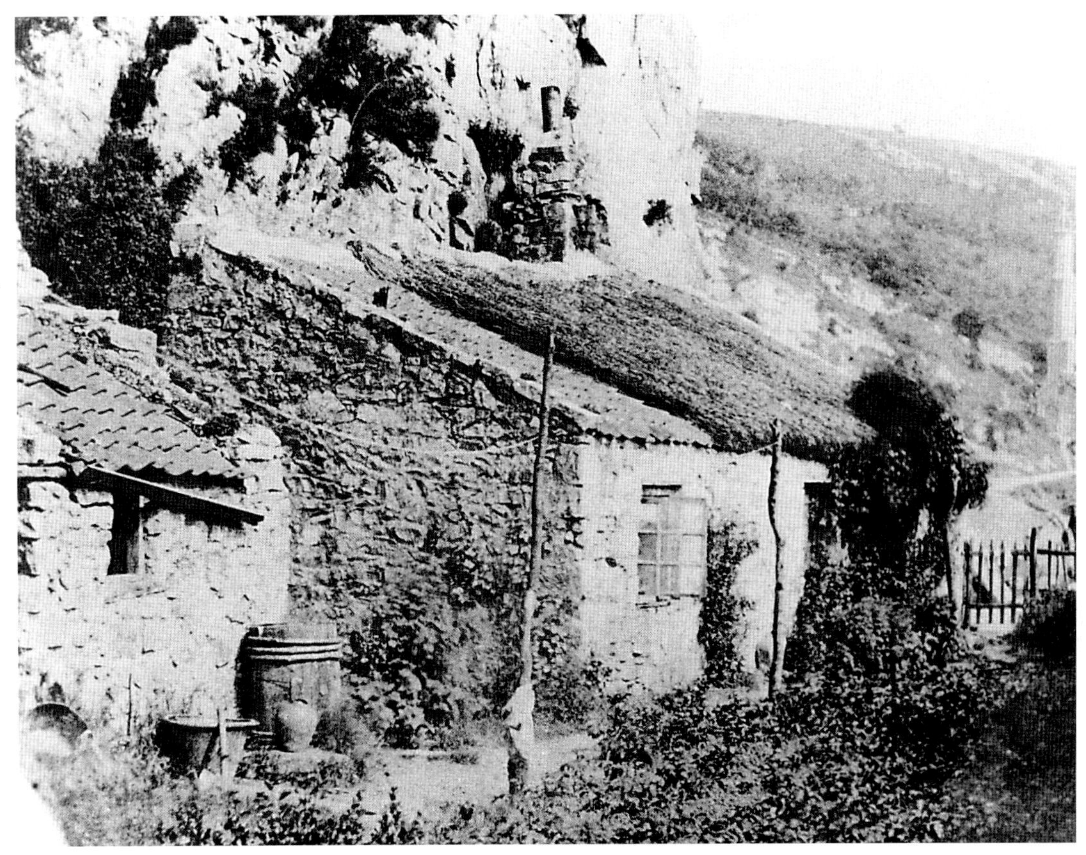

An early 1850s study of a small building at the foot of Sea Walls by John Bevan Hazard (died 1892). Isambard Kingdom Brunel's recently built Black Rock Pumping Station is seen in the background. The station, funded by the Merchant Venturers to supply fresh springwater to Clifton, was built in 1845 but demolished 20 years later for the construction of the Bristol Port Railway to Avonmouth.

Photo: Bristol Records Office

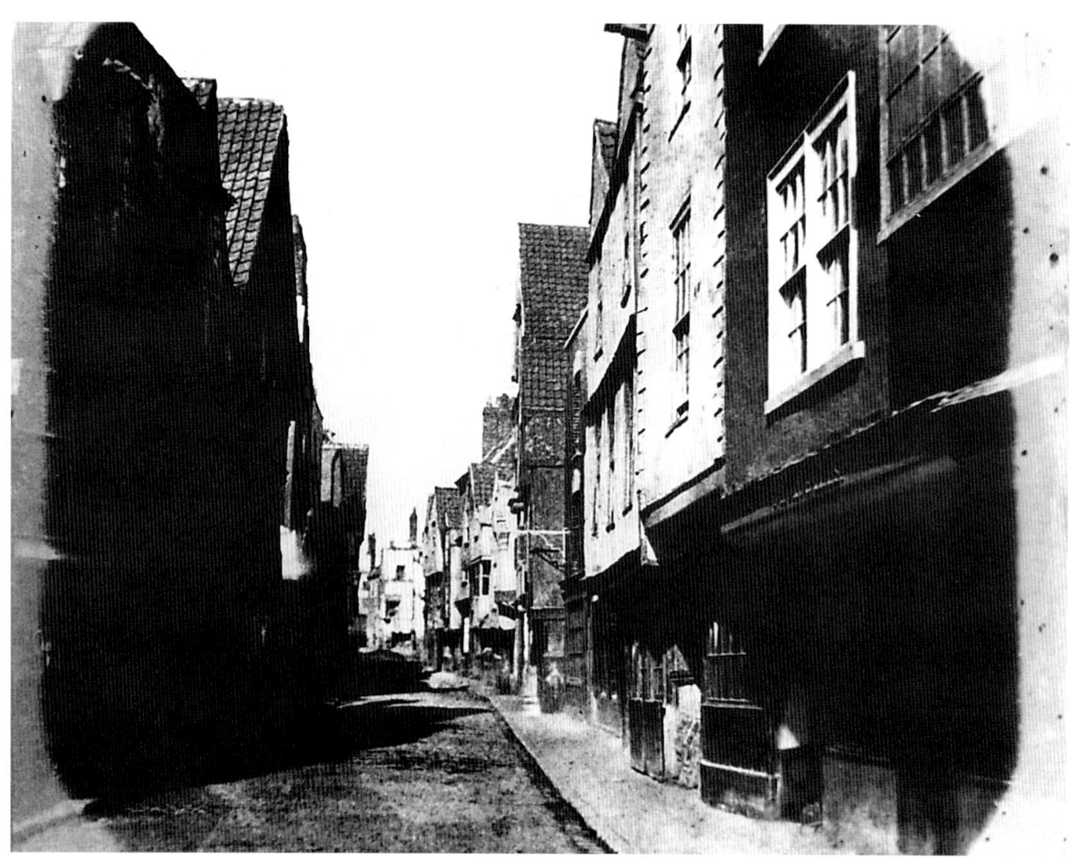

Lewin's Mead. In his early 1850s Calotype, Hugh Owen (1808-1897) made the most of the bright sunlight and deep shadows to capture the spirit of a Bristol that was to soon disappear. Many of the buildings had been cleared away within two decades.

Photo: Bristol Records Office

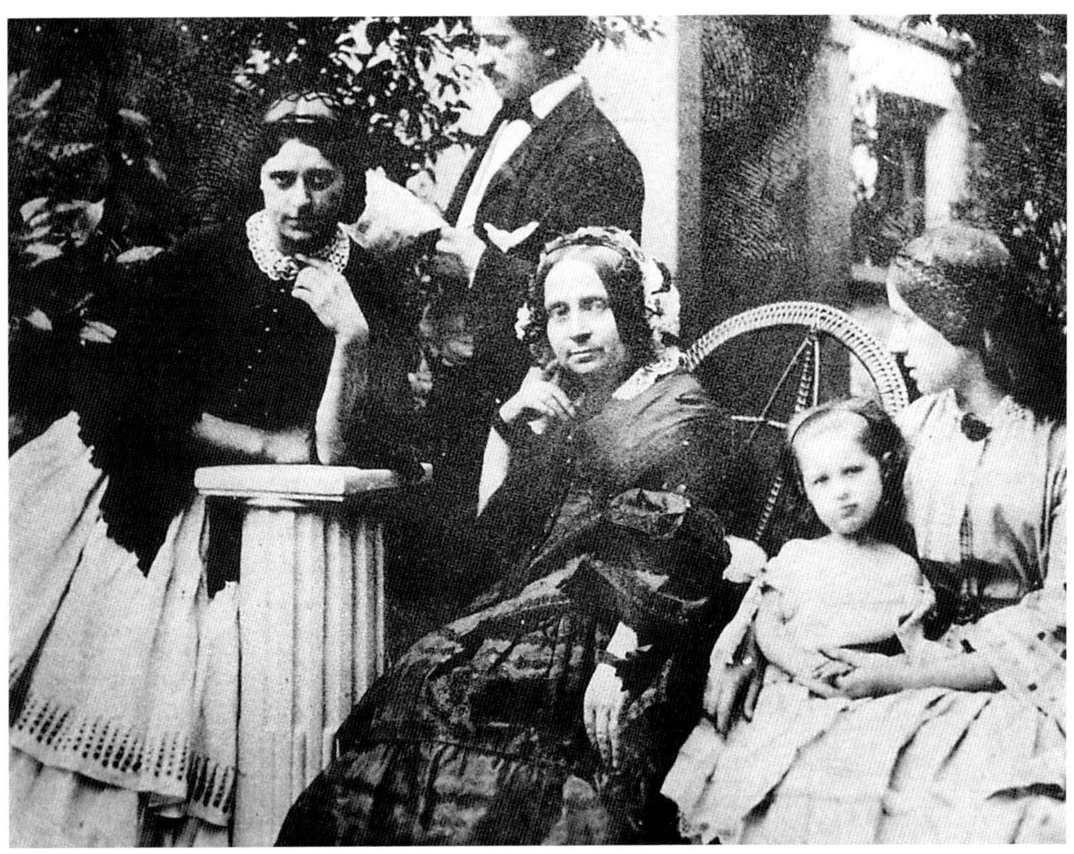

An obviously studied family grouping from the Fedden album, but this time with the camera set up as closely as possible to the subjects. The figures have adopted generous poses to fill the frame and form an elegant portraiture composition.

Photo: Bristol Records Office

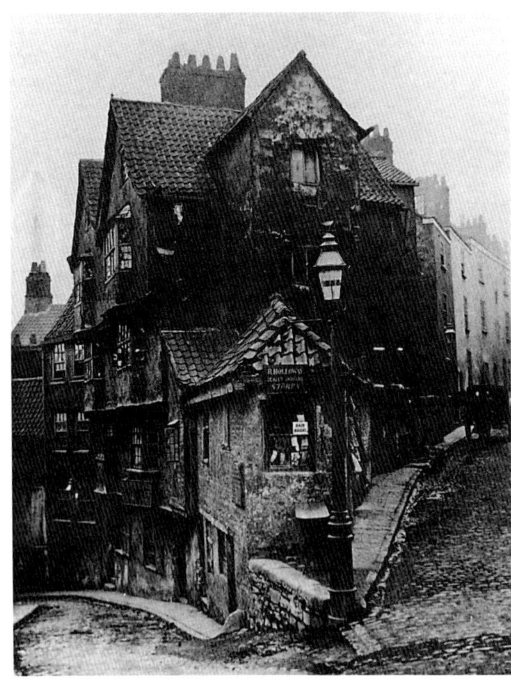

A deserted, cobbled Steep Street photographed in the 1860s. This particular olde worlde corner of Bristol was a favourite haunt of both artists and photographers and several near-identical views looking down Steep Street from Trenchard Street were made in the first two decades of photography.

Photo: Bristol Museums and Art Gallery

This provincial hesitance brought great benefits to the nostalgic lens of contemporary photographers - so a fair amount of the old Bristol lost to us has been inadvertently preserved.

The newly industrialised Victorians were enamoured of all things medieval, Gothic, Elizabethan or Jacobean. The clean, austere, reasoned elegance of Georgian and Regency architecture and design was far too close to them in time and they passionately rejected them in their quest for a colourful, idealised, legendary past.

Photography arrived just in the nick of time to record some of the most picturesque cobbled streets which lay to the north of the harbour in the city centre. Hugh Owen's and John Hazard's studies of the hauntingly atmospheric Steep Street and its neighbourhood are historic as well as aesthetic gems.

Within less than 20 years the area had been flattened. Victorian sentimentality for things olde worlde gave way to Victorian dynamic practicality when those picture-postcard houses were razed and a wide, clean Colston Avenue was built. What the viewer does not see is that behind those quaint facades were some of the most verminous, overcrowded and unhealthy slums in Britain.

The Victorians ruthlessly demolished some other cherished landmarks in the city, notably the famous Blackboy Inn at the top of Whiteladies Road which was pulled down to make way for an efficient new road lay-out, still known as Blackboy Hill.

Owen and his friends preserved for posterity scenes of the popular, thriving area around St Peter's Church in the Wine Street/Castle Street district which older Bristolians remember vividly as the heart of the old city. Standing on Castle Park today, it is hard to imagine the look and the feel of this part of Bristol before the bombs landed in the first great blitz of November 1940.

Opposite: The Black Boy Inn on Whiteladies Road, one of Bristol's best-known sights in Victorian times and the subject of many early photographs. The inn was demolished in 1874 to clear the way for the increasing road traffic and the new junction was given the name Blackboy Hill.

Photo: Bristol Museums and Art Gallery

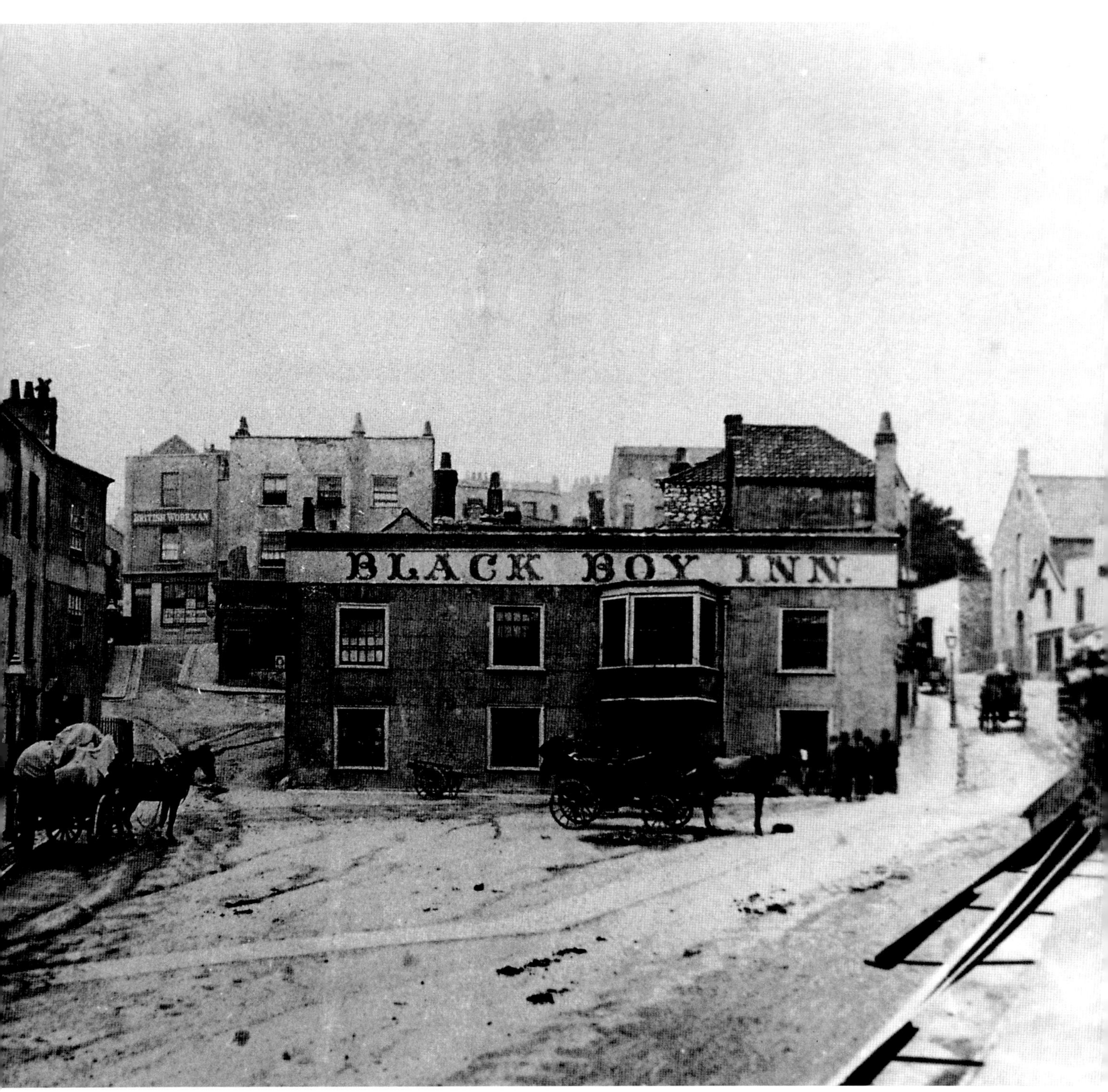
BRITISH WORKMAN
BLACK BOY INN.

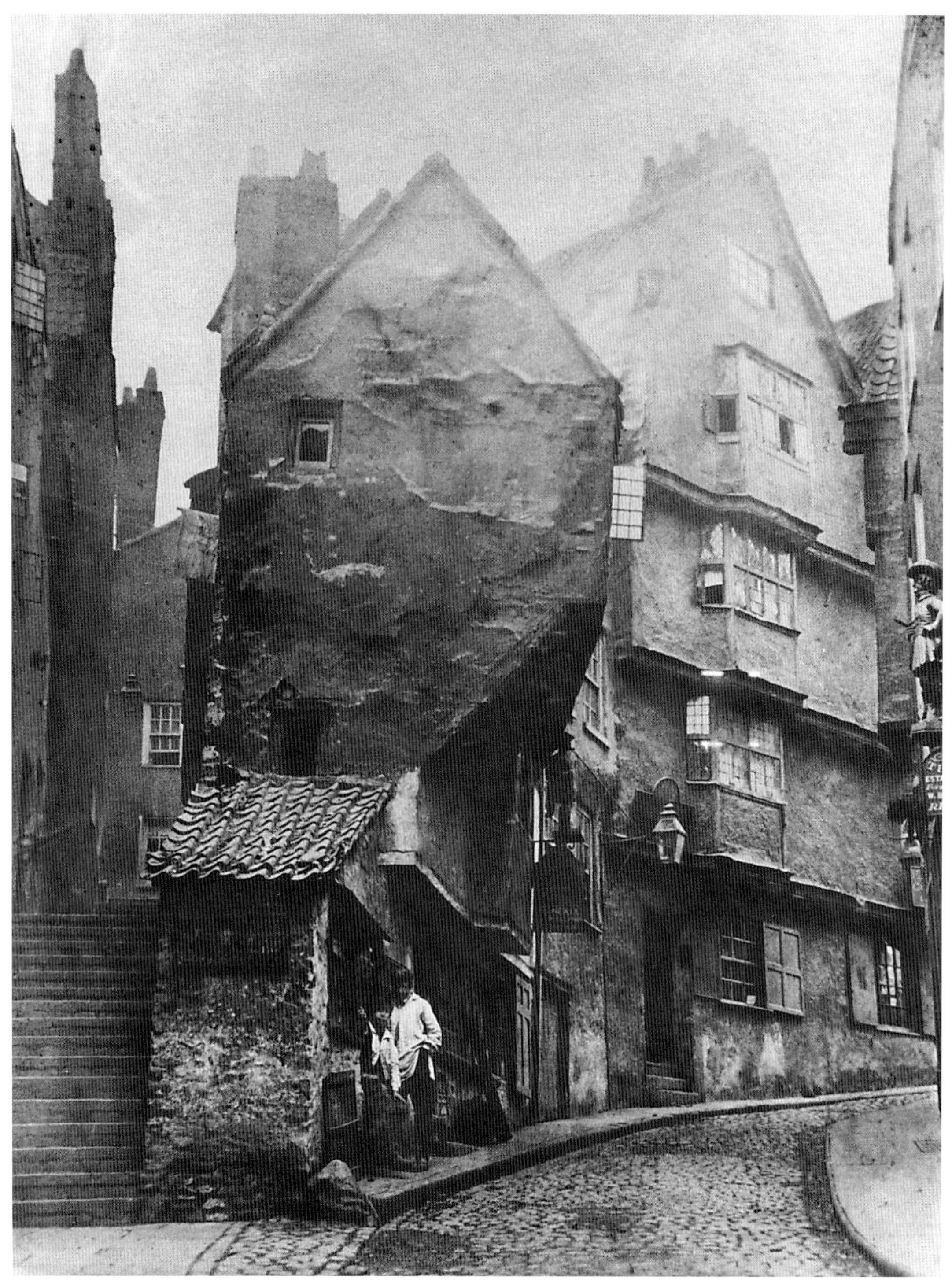

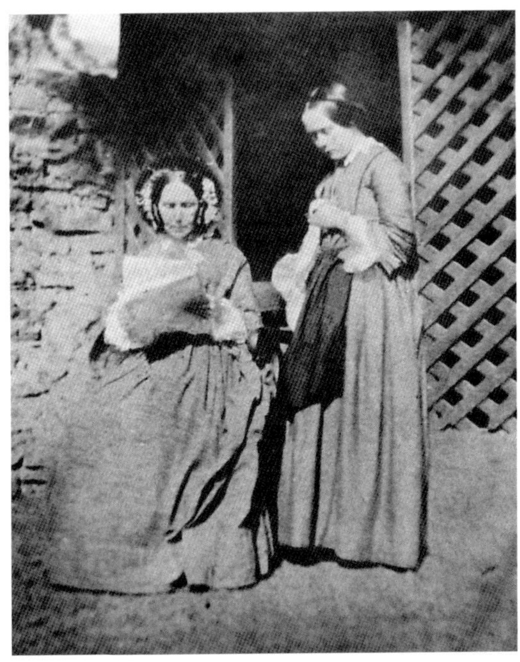 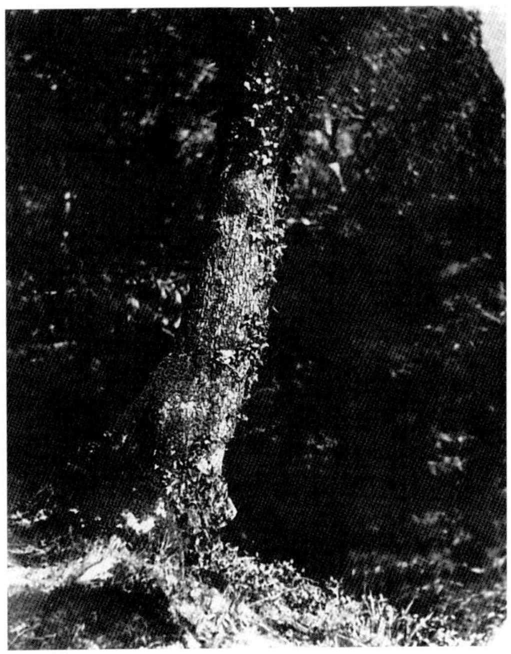

Above: Two women engrossed in their sewing, a picture from the Fedden family album, giving a homely glimpse into Victorian domestic life.

Photo: Bristol Records Office

Opposite: Steep Street, which would soon be cleared away and replaced by the broad, new road lay-out of Colston Avenue. These evocative facades and heavily shadowed streets just north of the city centre fascinated both artists and photographers although the grim reality was that behind these picturesque frontages lay some of the worst slums in Britain.

The slums were demolished in 1871.

Photo: Bristol Museums and Art Gallery

Above: A superb early Calotype of an ivy-clad tree in Leigh Woods, one of the treasures of the Fedden family album which was presented to the City of Bristol by Victor Fuller-Eberle. The attraction of the wild, rugged, natural beauty of Leigh Woods and the Avon Gorge was as powerful for the first photographers as it had been to the Bristol School of Artists a generation before.

Photo: Bristol Records Office

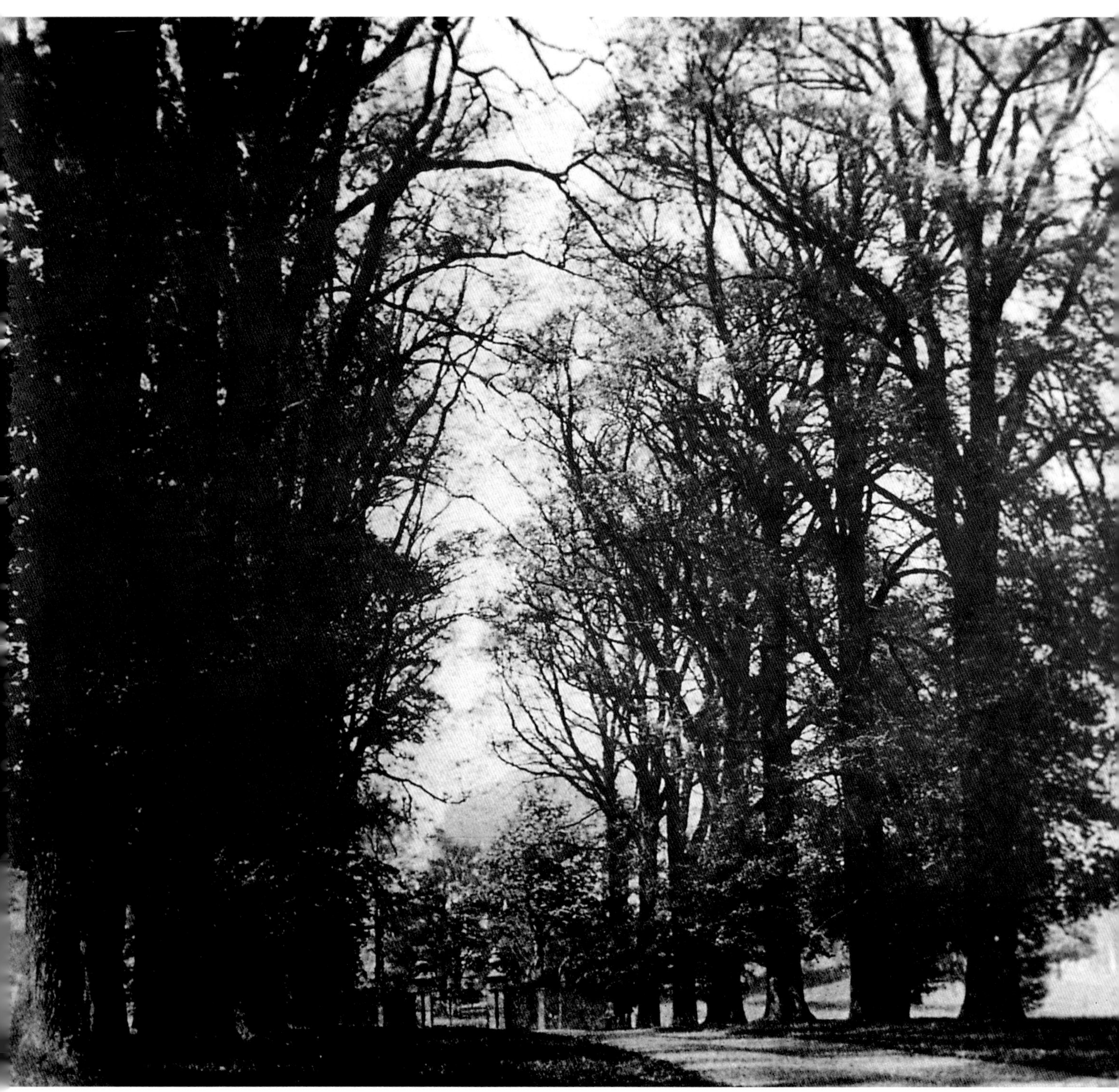

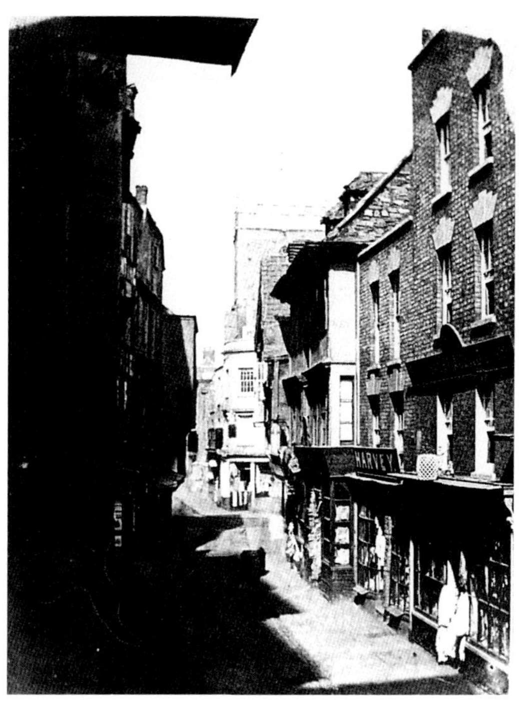

Above: Mary-Le-Port Street by Hugh Owen (1808-1897). This lively area, with St Peter's Church seen in the background, was once the heart of Bristol. Today the ruined church is left abandoned as a memorial to the Bristol blitzes and the site has become Castle Park.

Owen's early 1850s photograph was taken in daylight but the exposure time needed for this Calotype was so long that passers-by can only be dimly seen as ghostly images on the pavements.

Photo: Bristol Records Office

Opposite: Lovers Walk, Redland in the 1850s by John Bevan Hazard (died 1892). The avenue leads to Redland Court, now Redland High School for Girls. Hazard's delight in the delicate tracery of the lofty trees and the - to Victorian eyes - wealth of minute details which the magical art of photography offered is self-evident.

Photo: Bristol Records Office

Hugh Owen's pictures are a haunting, fixed historical record of a lost treasure.

Bristol was growing and its suburbs were becoming increasingly popular as the better-off citizens escaped the dirty, smoky, often smelly, congested city centre. These new havens offered a very desirable vision of urban living, a refined, unhurried city fringe where town and country merged almost imperceptibly.

This side of Victorian life is reflected in charming sequences of pictures, particularly of the Redland area where Lovers Walk, Redland Court and the delightful baroque Redland Chapel offered photographers a rosy vision of a passing era which they ardently captured on film.

The changing Bristol the early photographers knew was a delight. It offered so much . . . fine landscape, exciting architectural photography, genre studies of children, romantic townscapes and myriad street scenes. It was a city of great contrasts and on the brink of irrevocable change. They accepted the challenge adroitly and with enthusiasm.

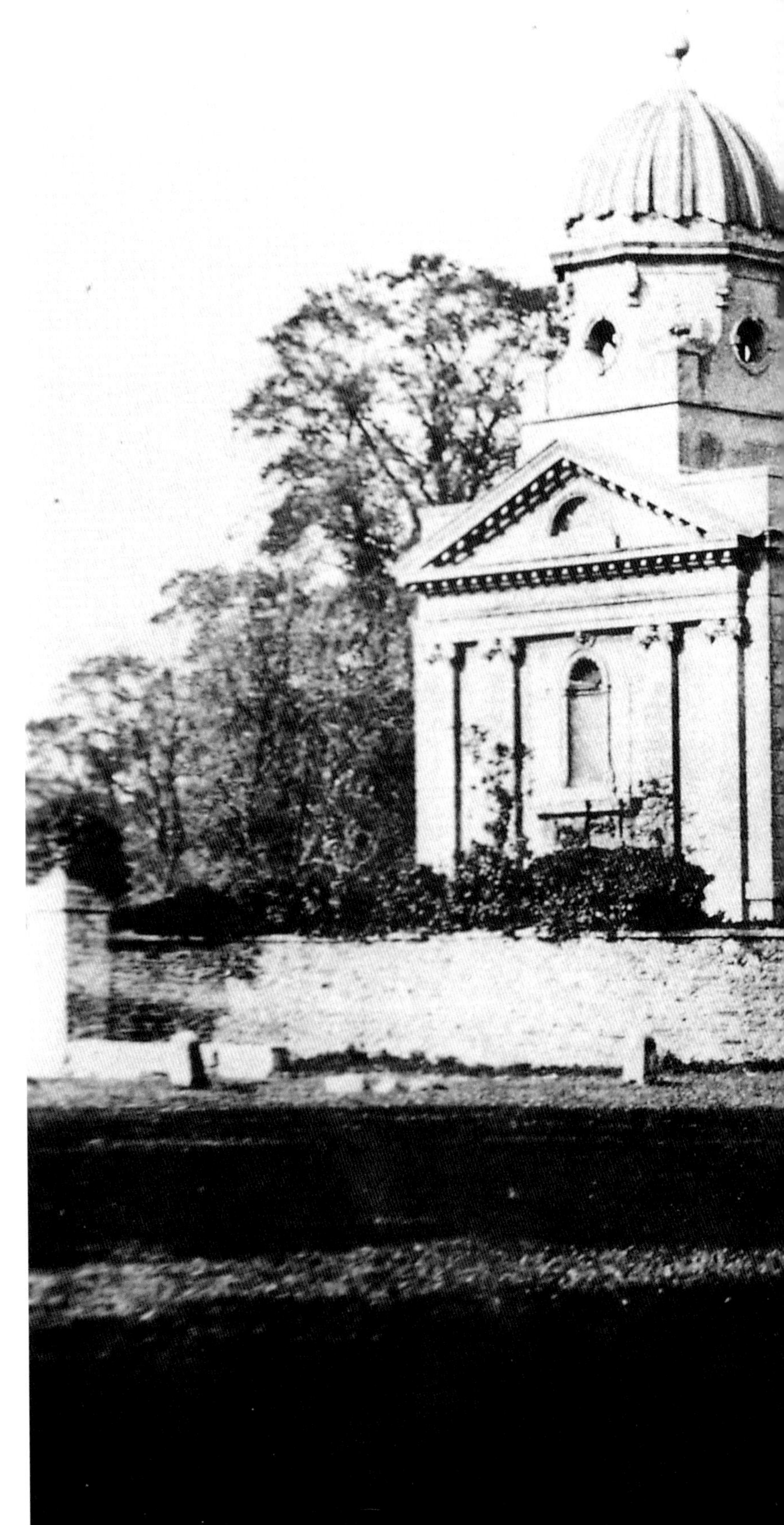

Redland Chapel in the 1850s. A deliberately artistic approach to the composition… the pose of the sitter gives a curiously 18th century feel to this picture.

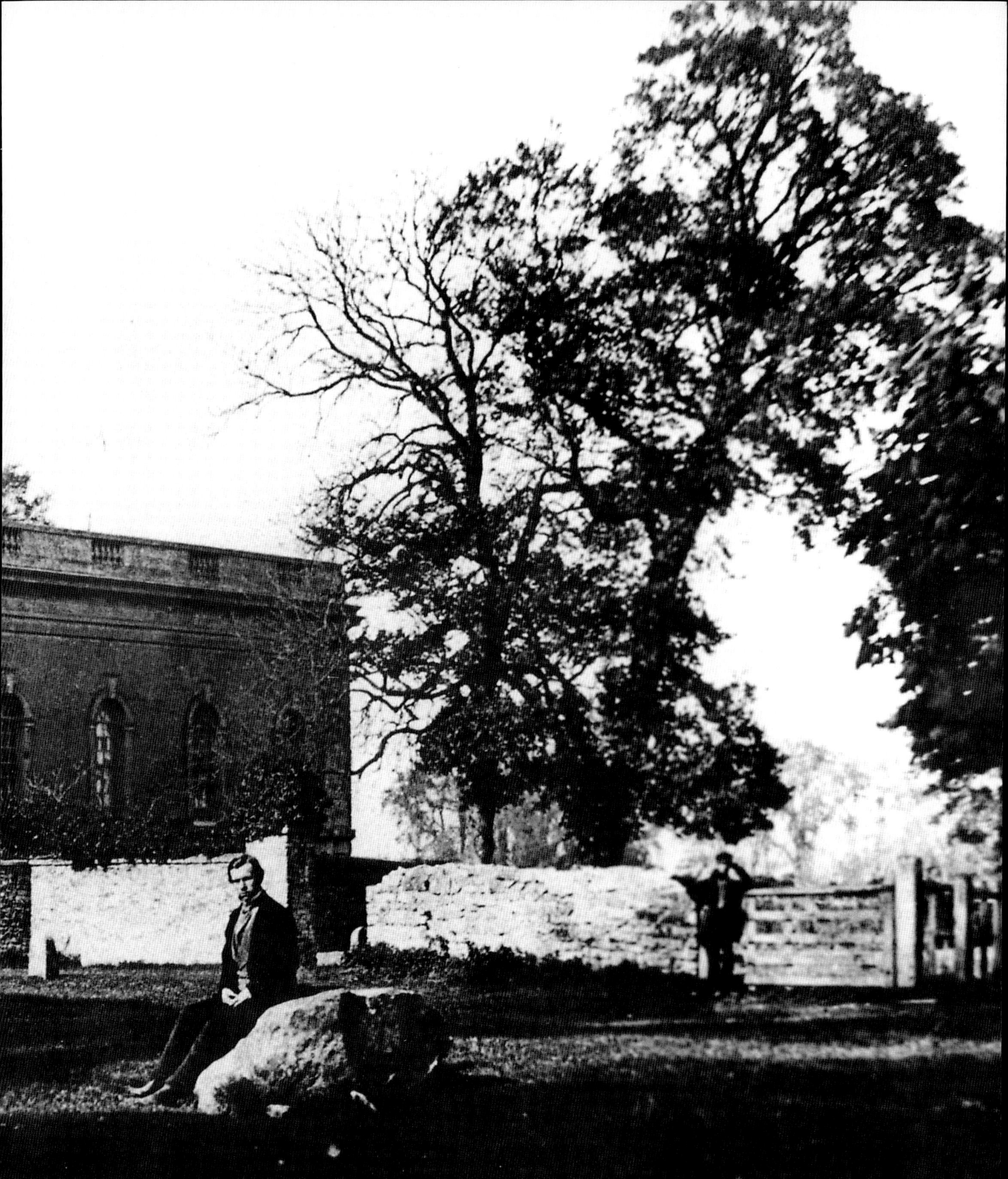

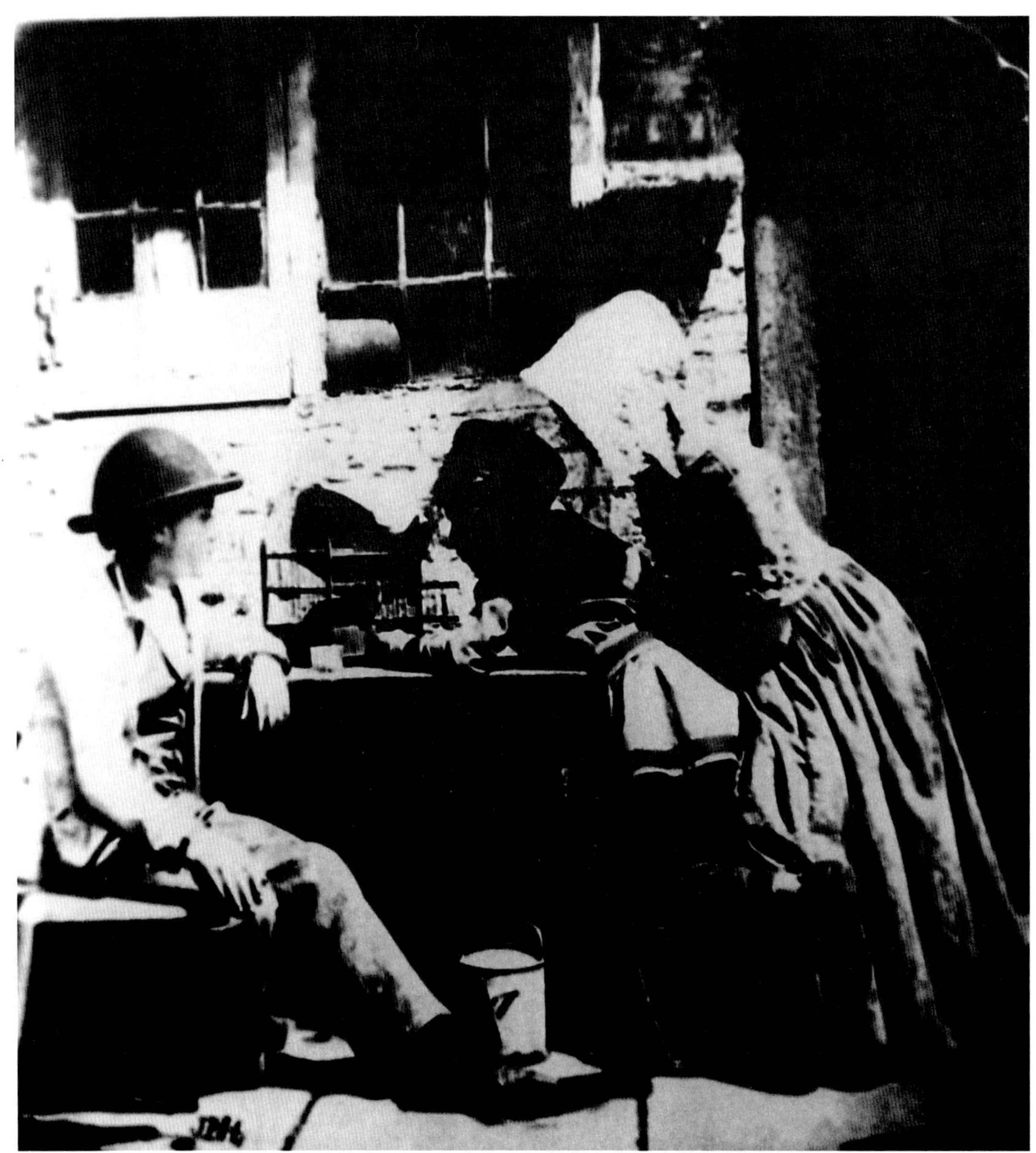

The Bird Cage by John Bevan Hazard (died 1892),
one of his many studies of children at play. Hazard
carefully arranged the poses which not only captured
the mood of concentration of the children but were
also comfortable enough for them to stay still for a
long time.

The boy in the hat also appears in the Marble Players
on page 84.

Photo: Bristol Records Office

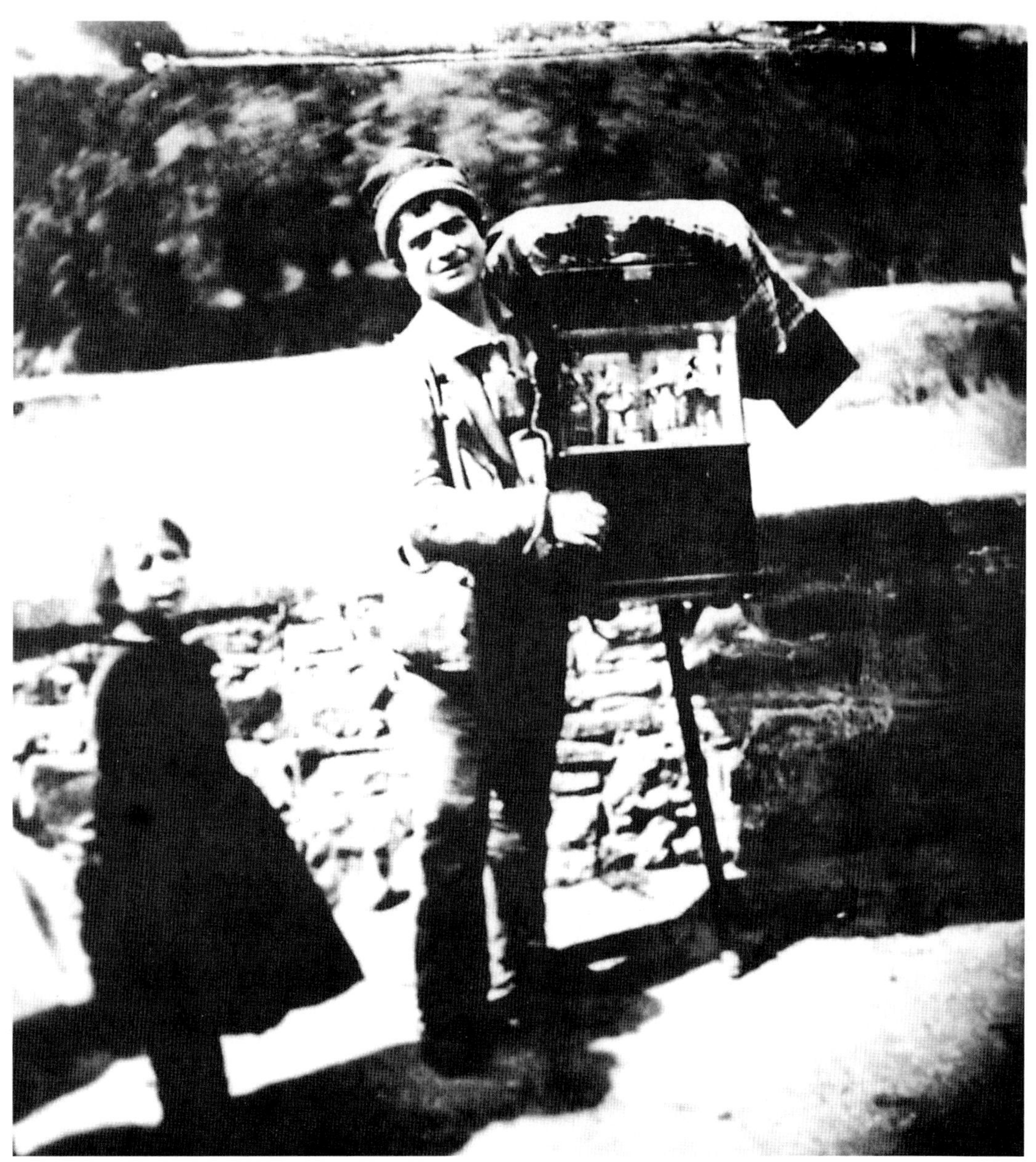

The Organ Grinder with his musical instrument balanced on a single supporting leg, photographed in Bristol in the 1850s. Street characters were popular subjects in Victorian literature and art and quickly became favourites for photographers too.

Photo: Bristol Records Office

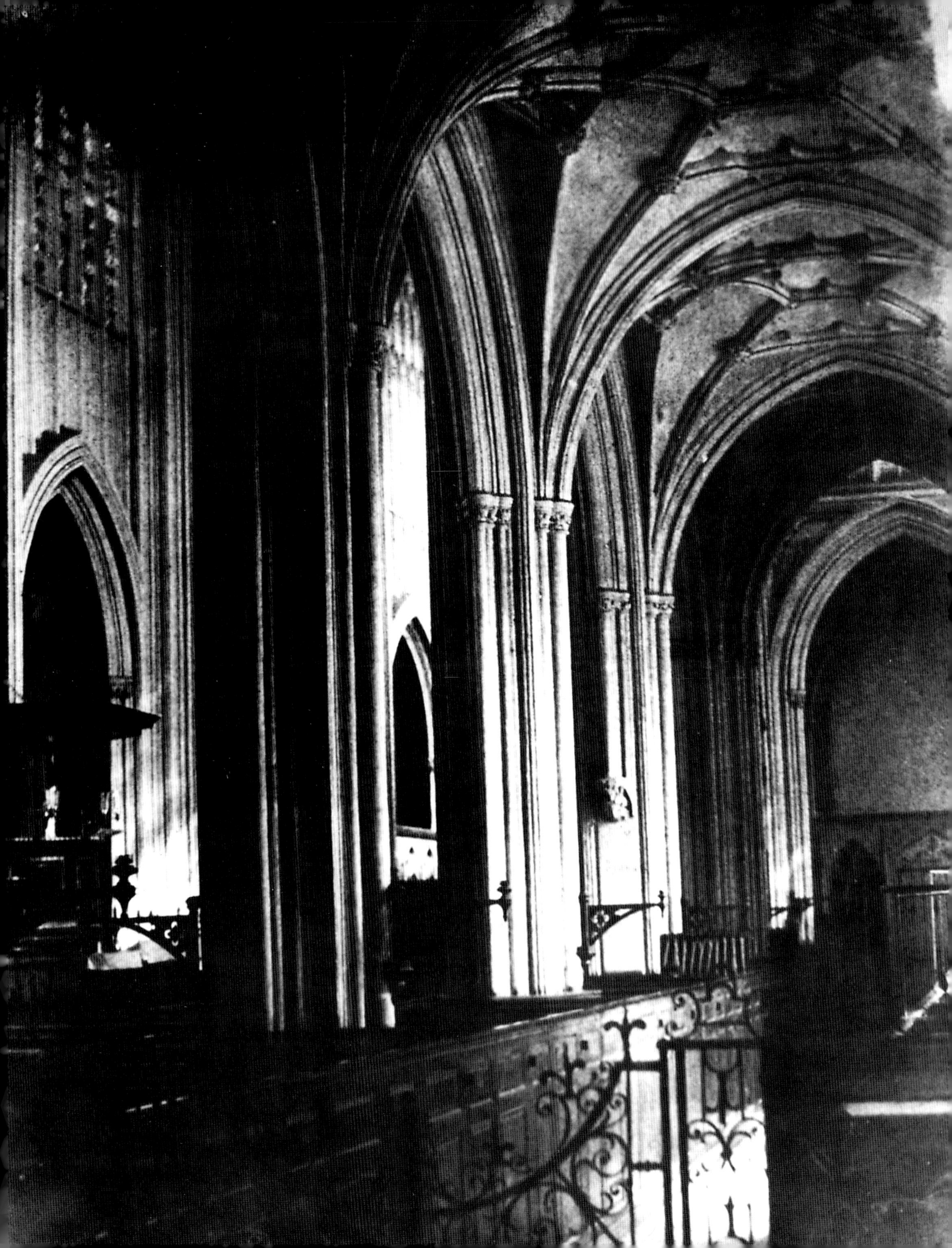

City of Artists

Bristol makes remarkably little play of its considerable role in that free-thinking, inspired, sometimes reckless world of the Romantic Movement - a movement which loosely drew together seemingly differing strands including poetry, art and early photography. It is a strange omission because both Bristol's medieval remains and unique landscape were important inspirations to some of the most famous and influential romantics of all.

Even today, as Bristol re-examines its past and re-assesses its signifance as a fascinating city which has played its part in the history of Western Europe, it continues to ignore one of the most quirky and colourful episodes in the Romantic canon . . . the true story of the brilliant, febrile young Bristol poet Thomas Chatterton (1752-1770). Chatterton single-handedly invented the powerful image of the doomed, neglected genius starving to death in a garret. His own agonised suicide - and his belated, growing legend - sparked an epidemic of copycat deaths among young people in Europe.

The boy Chatterton's inspiration was St Mary Redcliffe Church, which had been praised by Elizabeth I as "the fairest, goodliest and most famous parish church in England". His uncle was a sexton there and the adolescent was allowed to roam the building, examining the tombs and inscriptions, reading arcane manuscripts in the muniments room and basking in the hallowed atmosphere and architectural glory.

In his teens, Chatterton found fragments of old, blank parchments at the church. The romantic in him seized the opportunity. He perfected a mock-medieval literary style, invented a new persona for himself in the form of a 15th century poet-priest Thomas Rowley, who lived at the time of the great Bristol merchant William Canynge, and began to write epic, glittering poems.

He presented these to a Bristol publisher who was fooled. When the "Rowley" poems appeared, they caused a great stir and although the deception was discovered, the boy wonder was so pleased with his offbeat literary success that he moved to London, where he felt his precocious talents would be better rewarded. Instead he found indifference, disillusionment and poverty. He poisoned himself in an attic in 1770 aged 17.

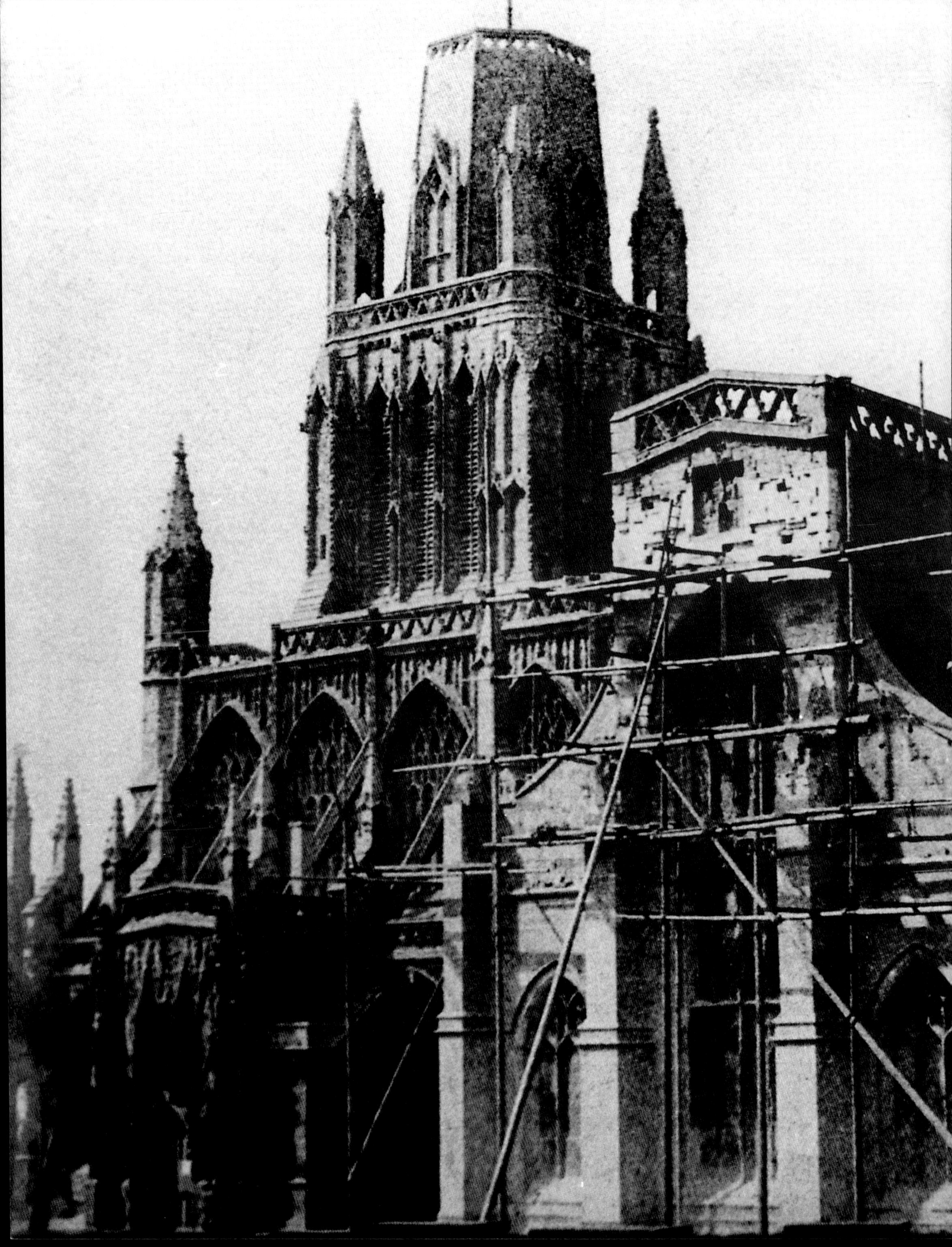

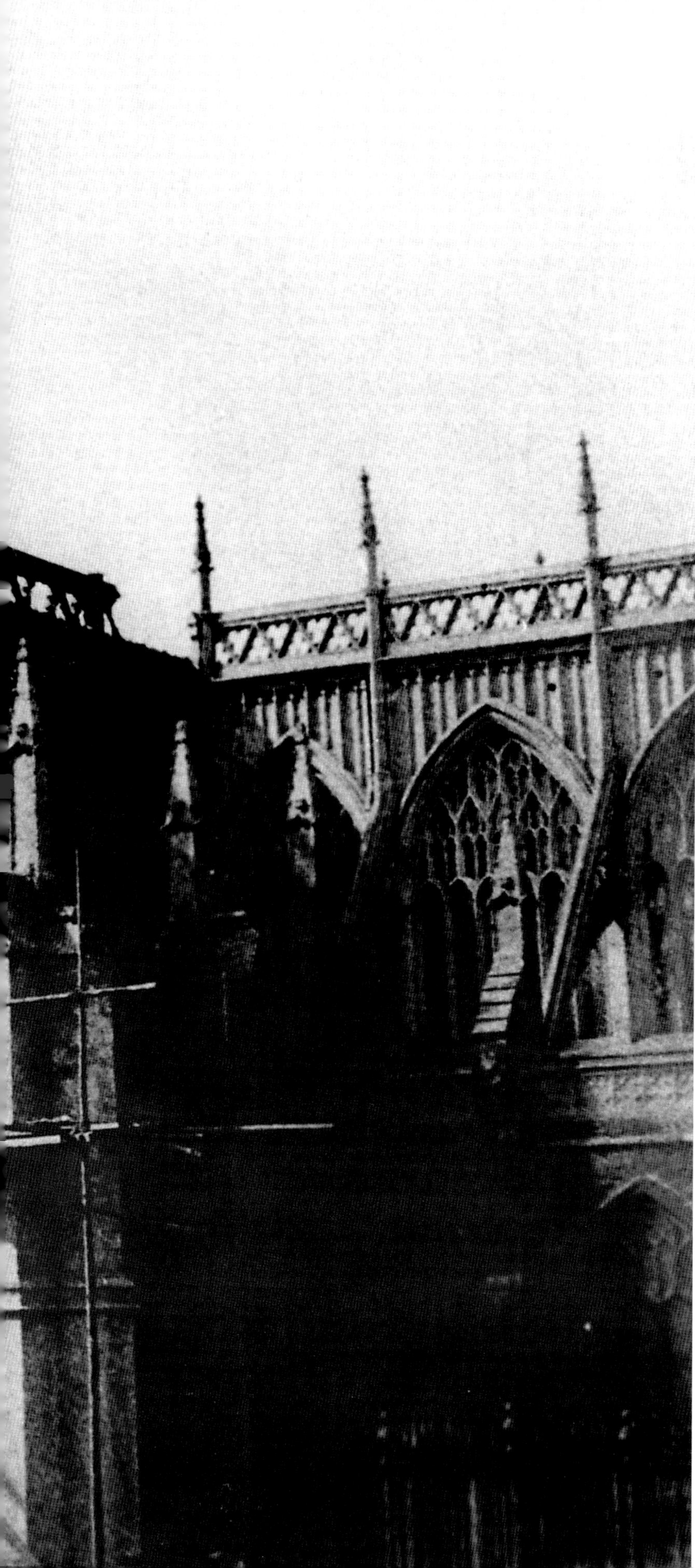

St Mary Redcliffe Church by John Bevan Hazard (died 1892). Hazard was the latest in a long line of devoted admirers of St Mary Redcliffe Church when he took this picture during the restoration of the south transept in 1855. The church, praised by Elizabeth I, had inspired the poets Thomas Chatterton (1752-1770) and Samuel Taylor Coleridge (1772-1834) and many painters, local and national. Hugh Owen (1808-1897), like Coleridge, was married at St Mary Redcliffe.

Photo: Bristol Records Office

It is difficult to exaggerate the sensational effect this affair had on young people not just in the years shortly after his death but in the centuries which followed. You still hear echoes of it today in the mythology surrounding young rock and film stars who die tragically unfulfilled. Chatterton created the mould.

The great, recognised Romantic poets Keats, Coleridge, Wordsworth, Southey and Shelley were obsessed by his legend. It was no coincidence that Coleridge chose to hold his wedding at St Mary Redcliffe in 1795, a quarter of a century after Chatterton's death, and he was moved to tears by thoughts of his driven young hero prowling the building where the ceremony took place.

Wordsworth wrote:

"I thought of Chatterton, the marvellous Boy
The sleepless Soul that perished in his pride"

Chattertonmania was not confined to Britain. The Italians caught Chatterton fever with a successful tragic opera. In France a melodrama based on the story caused a furore when starry-eyed teenagers began killing themselves a la Chatterton and even today the boy poet is far more celebrated in France than he is in his native city.

The end of the 18th and the early years of the 19th century might have been a watershed in Bristol's commercial history, marking the start of the rapid decline of trade in the city docks, but the period was a particularly exciting one for an artistic community creating a golden age inspired by Chatterton. The visionary young Samuel Taylor Coleridge set up an idealistic community on College Green in 1794 with friends including Robert Southey, later to become Poet Laureate. Coleridge met and formed a close friendship with William Wordsworth in Bristol. The uneasy spirit of Chatterton and the awe-inspiring St Mary Redcliffe Church had a profound effect on all of them. But it was not only Bristol's gothic treasures which so excited and drove the new Romantics… it was also the extraordinary landscape which surrounded them.

These young idealists were rejecting the old order of the 18th century with its mannered elegance, its artificial landscapes created by Capability Brown and other great gardeners, its love of classical order and its calm, certain rule of Reason. They wanted stronger meat and drink in everything they did - and they found it in Bristol. They experimented with drugs and gases to transport themselves to new highs. They explored and enjoyed the large, exciting nautical city with its underlying radical spirit - and disported themselves in a landscape which could have been tailor-made for them.

Within a short walk of the city centre they could discover and lose themselves in utterly different worlds - scaling or admiring the great crags of the Avon Gorge, picnicing across the river in the leafy sanctuary of Leigh Woods, meandering along the wooded Frome or striding across the bracing Downs escarpment, all of them places of wild, natural beauty. Coleridge and his poetic friends were great walkers and admirers of nature at its most spectacular, as were the painting fraternity.

The painter Edward Bird (1772-1819) was among the first of the artistic newcomers and he was as delighted as the poets by both Bristol's medieval buildings and its compellingly dramatic surrounding landscape. He became the leader of a small, active group of professional and amateur artists which was to develop into the Bristol School.

The Irish-born Francis Danby (1793-1861) followed in 1813 and quickly established himself by specialising in picturesque paintings of the Avon Gorge. He, too, discovered Leigh Woods and he was so thrilled by the place that he made it a sort of aesthetic yardstick when judging other people's sensibilities.

He once said of his fellow Bristol School of Artists painter and friend Samuel Jackson:
"I know Jackson is a man of genius by being with him in Leigh Woods." He made a similar remark about another artist after "a day in Leigh Woods with him which is an excellent place for painters to become acquainted."

Opposite: The great Norman arch at College Square, a subject which fascinated photographers in an age enraptured by medievalism and the fashion for Gothic revival. The camera's closeness to the archway gives a wealth of detail of the carving while deep shadows give a funnelled glimpse of the view beyond.

Photo: Bristol Museums and Art Gallery

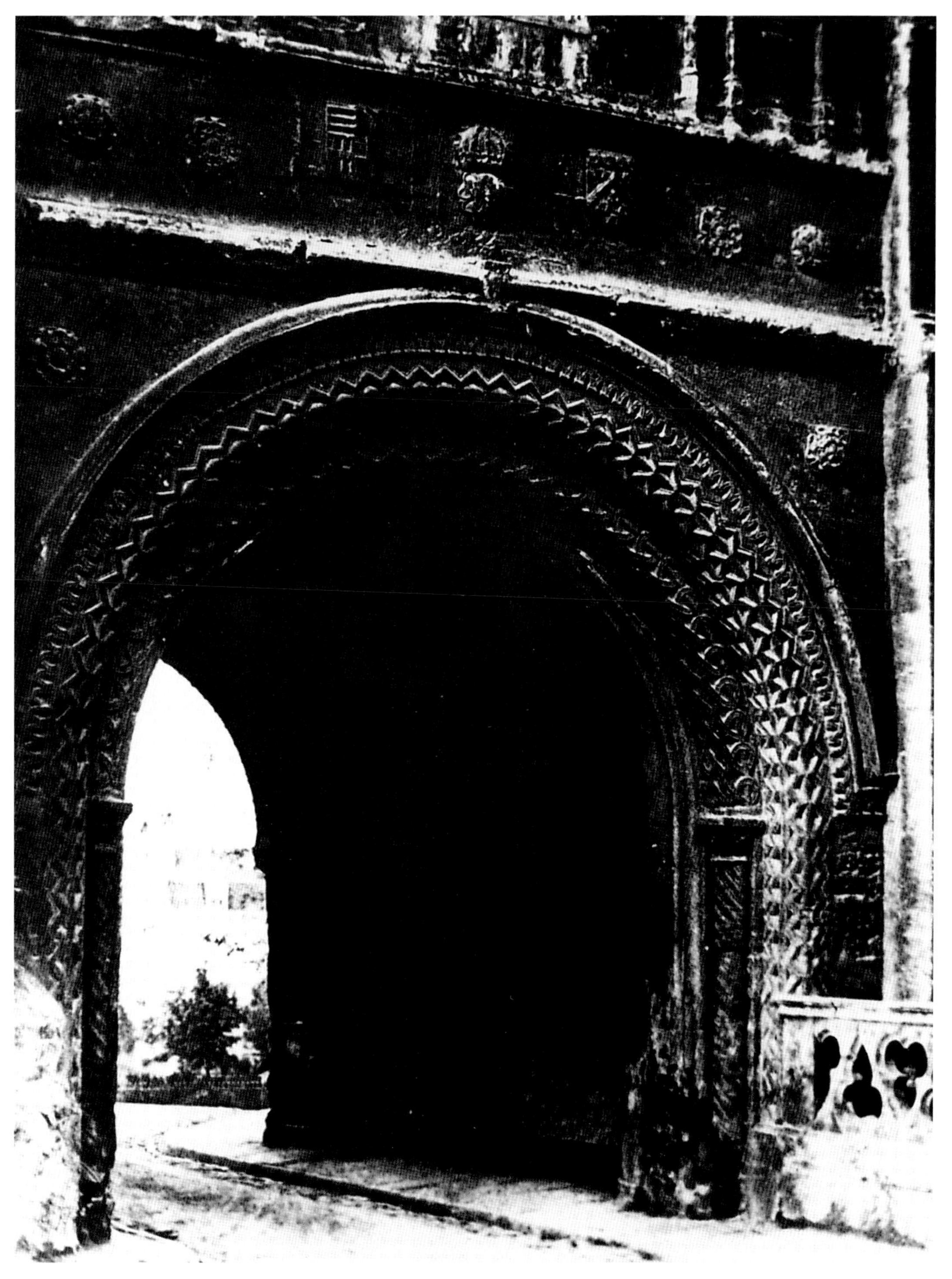

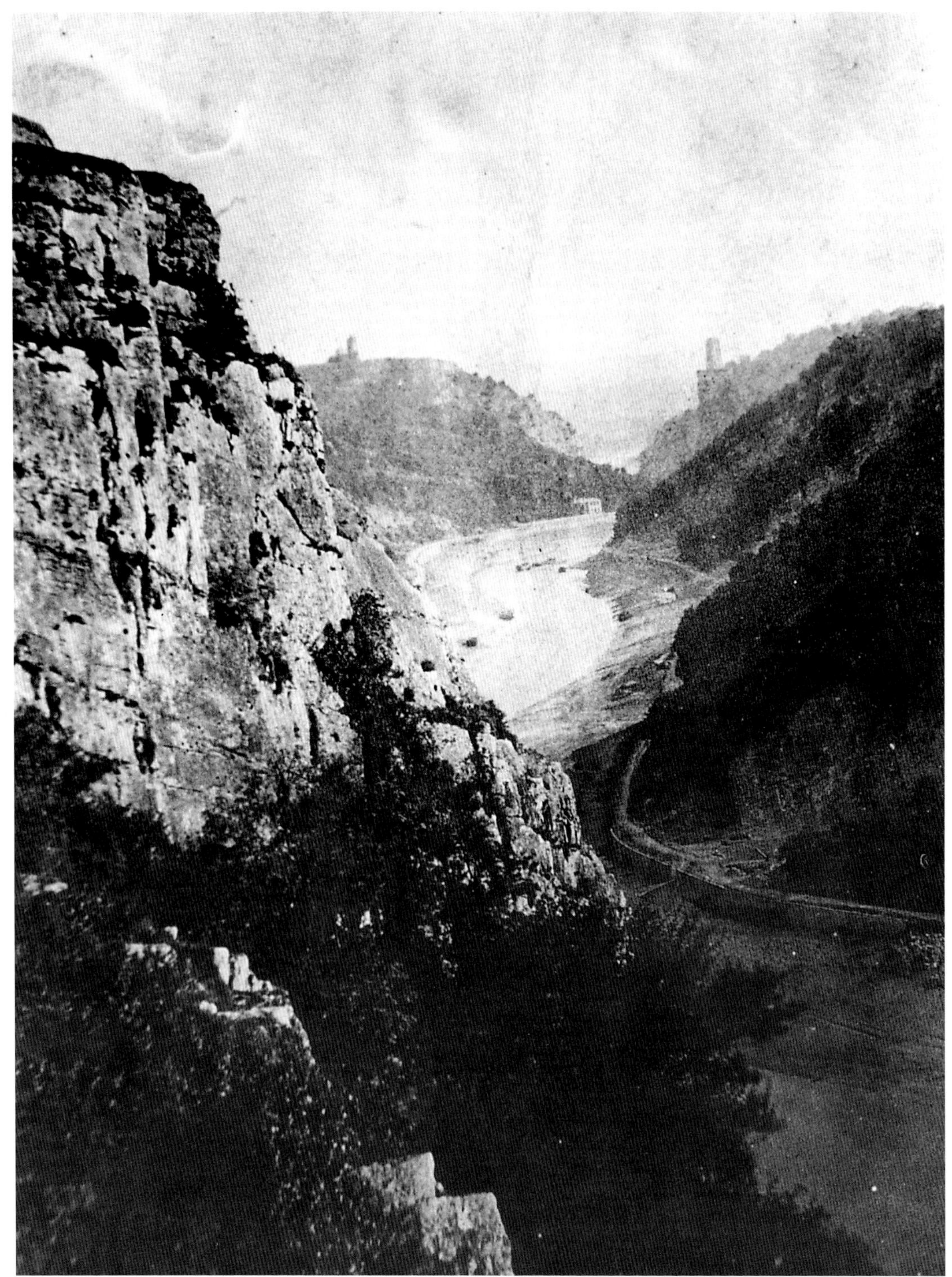

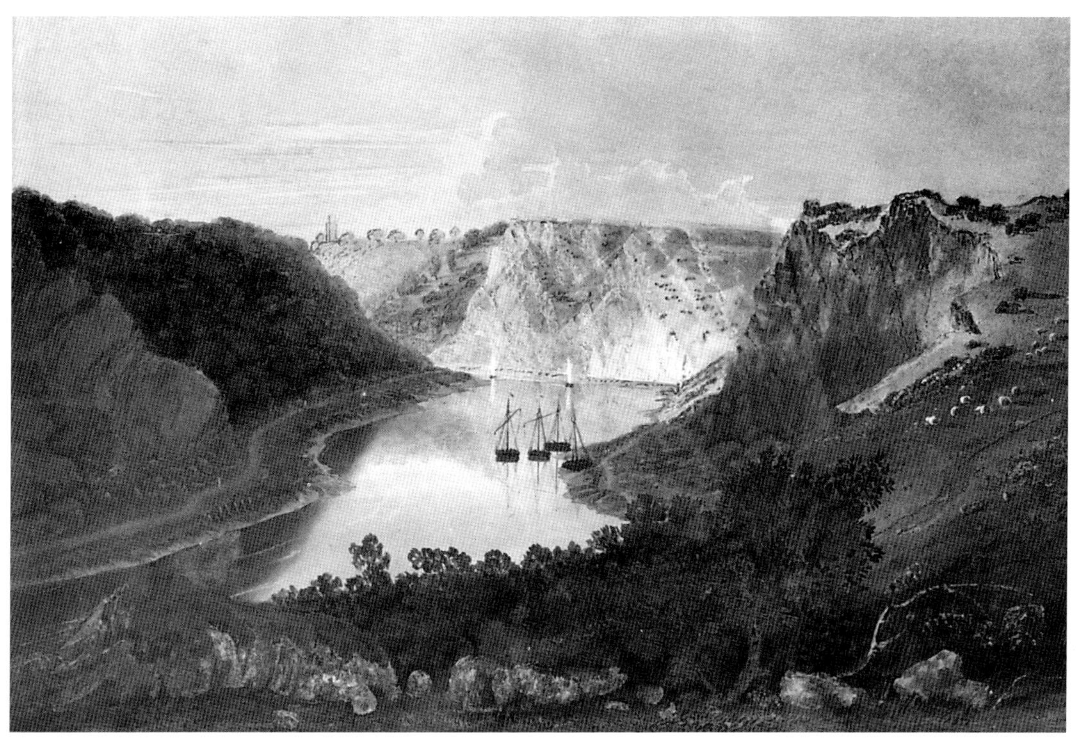

Above and opposite: The drama of the Avon Gorge was a recurring theme for the Bristol School of Artists. Samuel Jackson (1794-1869) painted The Avon Gorge At Sunset in about 1825, a beautiful study of the cliffs and wooded hillsides. The flat-bottomed quarry barges await the limestone which was used for building houses, walls, repairing roads and even as ships' ballast.

Capturing the scene in the first photographs 25 to 30 years later was not an easy task but this 1850s depiction succeeds admirably.

Watercolour: Bristol Museums and Art Gallery

Photo: Bristol Records Office

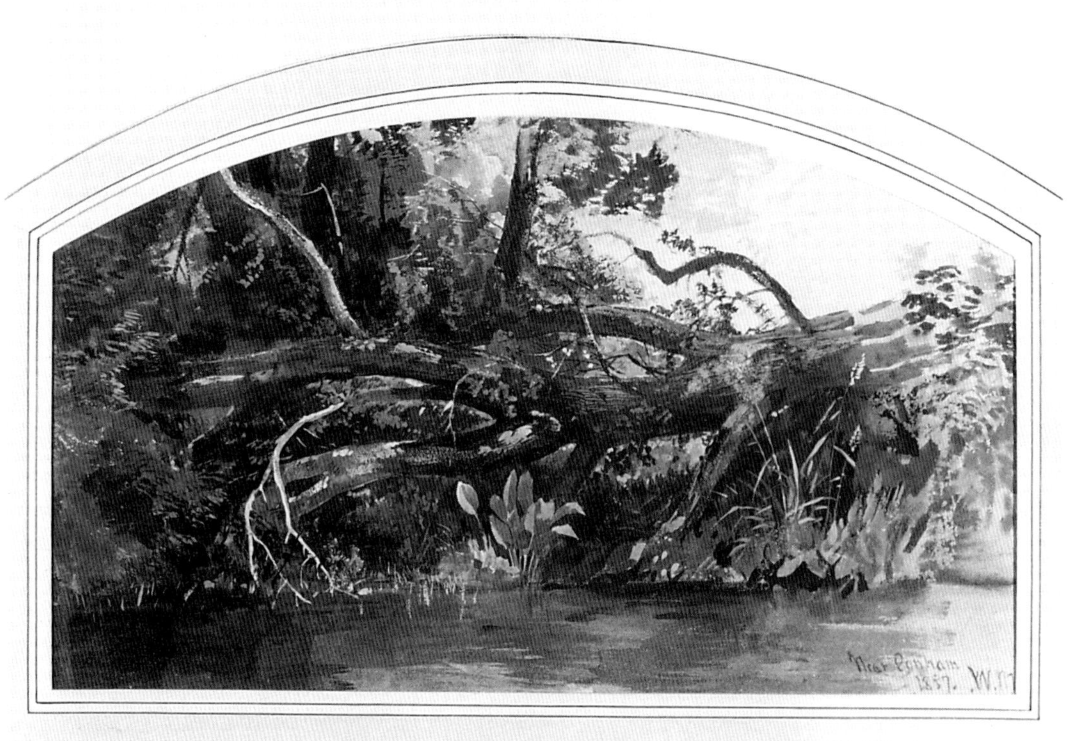

Above: Near Conham by W.J. Muller (1812-1845), a woodland scene between Bristol and Hanham, has shade set against light emphasising the variety and density of the greens. Understated, creative use of light was one of the first lessons the early photographers learnt from the painters.

Watercolour: Bristol Museums and Art Gallery

Opposite: Pollarded oak trees in Leigh Woods. This ancient woodland was a favourite haunt of poets and painters. The painter Francis Danby (1793-1861) once remarked of his friend and painting companion Samuel Jackson (1794-1869) that "I know Jackson is a man of genius by being with him in Leigh Woods". Hugh Owen (1808-1897), John Bevan Hazard (died 1892) and their friends in turn clearly shared their enthusiasm and found the area a continuing source of inspiration.

Other arcadias which attracted the painters and the photographers in the Bristol region were the Frome Valley and the Avon further up-river, particularly the wooded areas between Bristol and Hanham.

Photo: Bristol Records Office

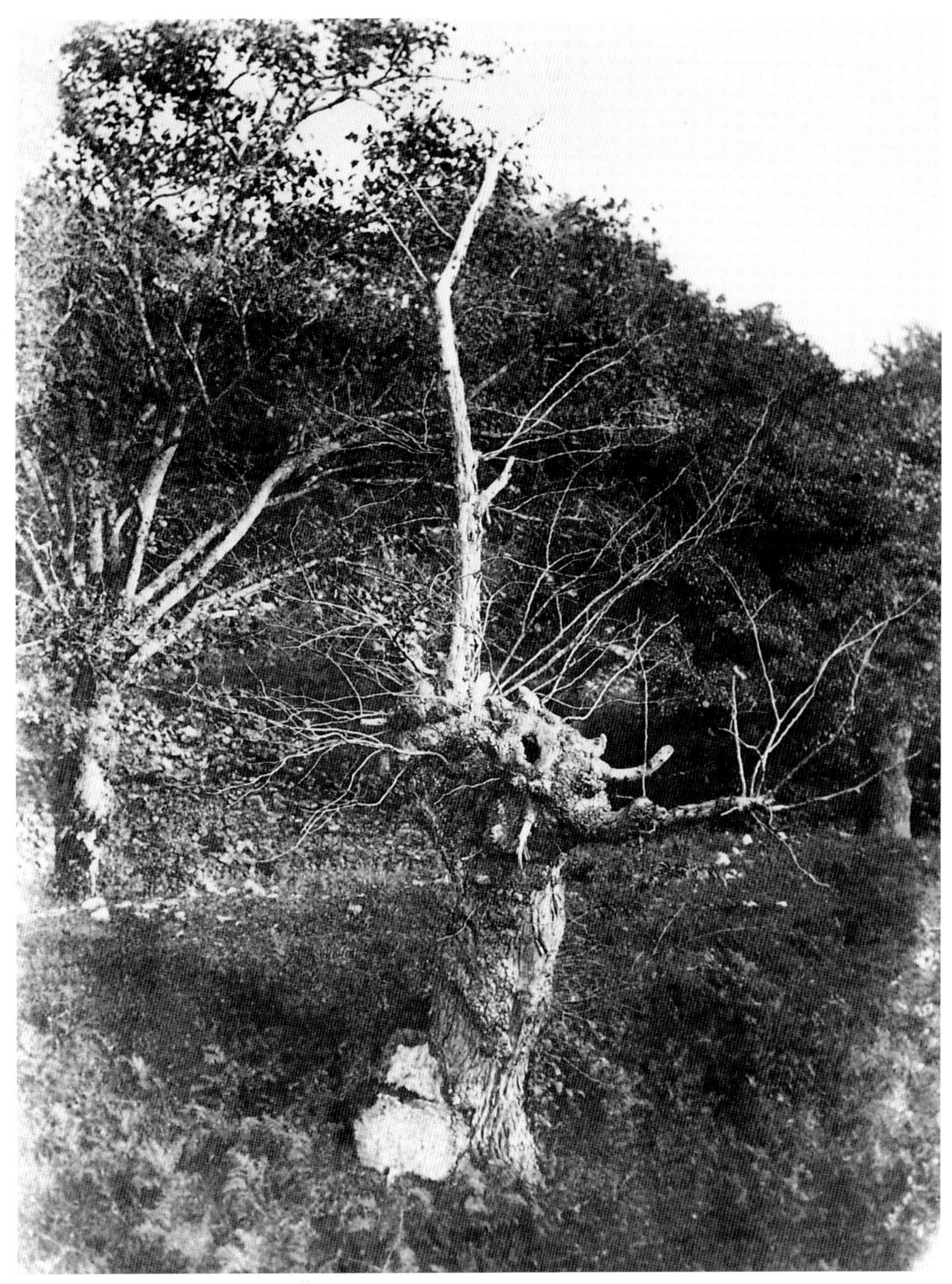

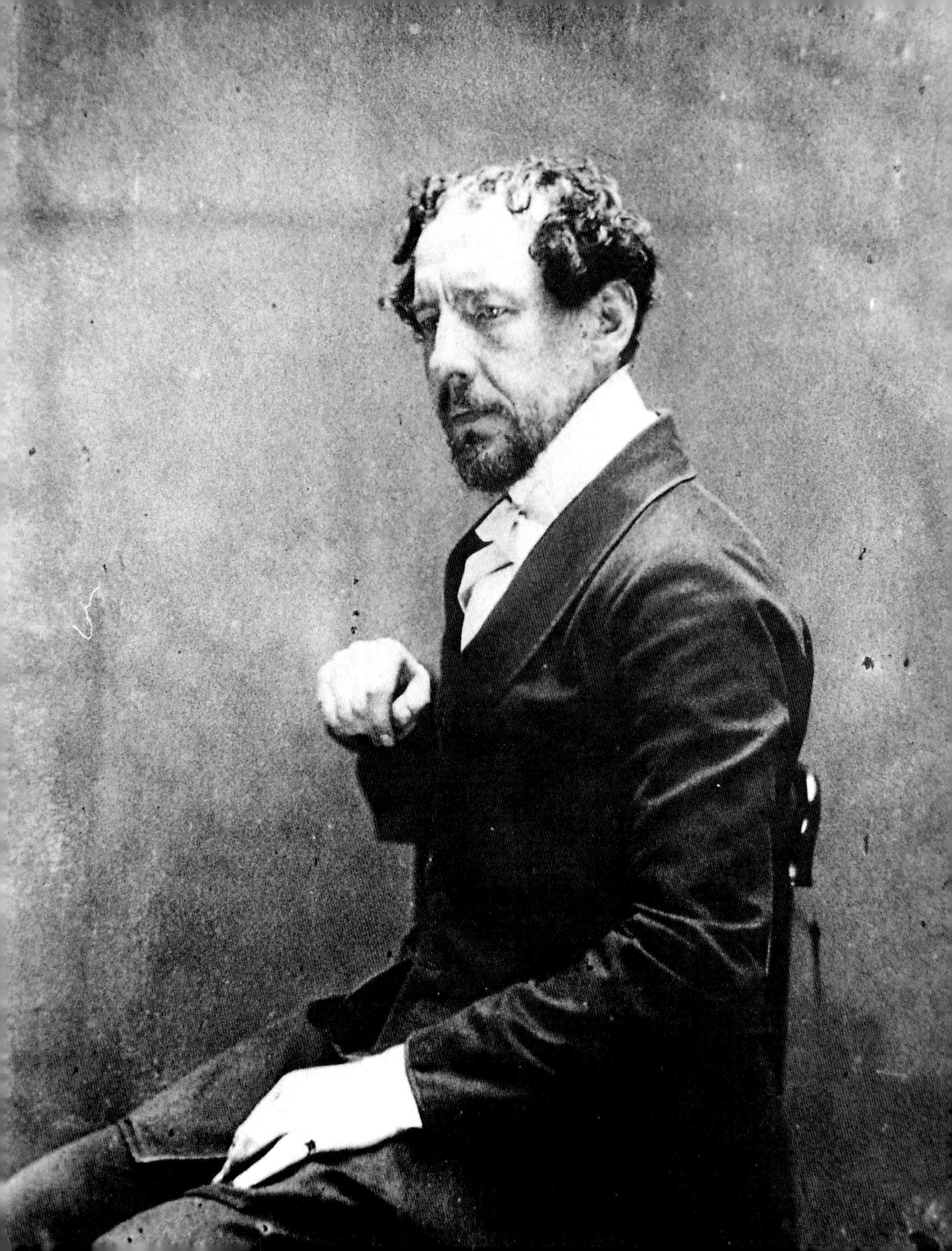

There is an equally effusive description of a
solitary visit to Leigh Woods by the amateur
artist, art patron and writer George Cumberland
(1754-1848), who once tellingly wrote about
Bristol: "I never enjoyed landscape till I came here
nor understood it".

He continued: "I rose at 5 o'clock and set off
alone for a walk to avoid the great heats . . . I
crossed the ferry, wound up the happy valley
reading Dante's Paradiso, and setting down at
each shady tree, it was then 7 o'clock and the
rabbits ran about like tame ones." He also, like
his friends, relished the more intimate beauty of
the wooded Frome Valley, which he painted.

For Samuel Jackson (1794-1869), the river
Avon, the Avon Gorge and the great sweep of the
Downs and views from Clifton and the Sea Walls
were some of Bristol's greatest attractions, and he
painted them repeatedly. His series of beautiful
watercolours pay tribute to a landscape which
deeply affected 19th century feelings and nurtured
the Victorian passion for the rugged and the
natural which later received the Royal blessing in
Queen Victoria's lasting love affair with the
scenery of Scotland.

Jackson was still very active in Bristol at the
dawn of photography and his work would have
been very well known to the city's first
photographers - one of them, after all, was his son
S.P. Jackson (1830-1904).

Following in the footsteps of the poets and
artists, it was now the photographers' turn to

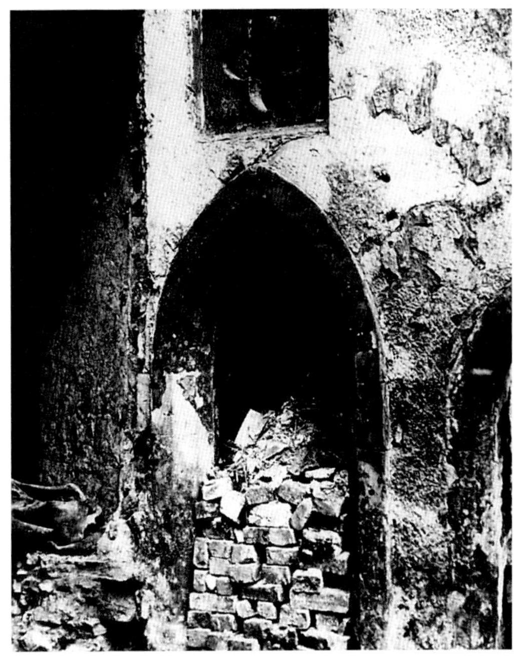

This strangely evocative study of a bricked-up
archway shows that the first Bristol photographers
grasped that their new art form offered many
opportunities for forceful, almost abstract
compositions.

Photo: Bristol Records Office

Opposite: Hugh Owen (1808-1897), photographed at
about the time he took his beautiful studies of Bristol
and the surrounding countryside. Owen, Chief Cashier
of the Great Western Railway, was one of early
photography's outstanding figures and a founder of
the first national photographic society alongside the
great Roger Fenton.

He was chosen by his peers as one of the two official
photographers of the Great Exhibition of 1851 and
bound volumes of his work were presented to Queen
Victoria and Prince Albert. Sadly, he abandoned
photography after less than 10 years because of his
dislike of the stains on his fingers caused by the
chemicals used in later photographic processes.

Photo: Bristol Records Office

explore identical subjects with their revolutionary
new processes.

Hugh Owen (1808-1897) was the most inspired
of all and if Danby is the senior talent of the
Bristol School of Artists, Owen was the master of
Bristol's early school of photographers. He shared
Coleridge's and Chatterton's love for St Mary
Redcliffe and, like Coleridge, was married in the
church. But unlike those radical poets, he was a
respectable member of the Bristol establishment.
His first wife was the daughter of a former
Master of the Merchant Venturers and he worked
in the very senior position of Chief Cashier of the
Great Western Railway. One of the advantages of
his post was that it involved regular train journeys
to London.

Owen knew William Fox Talbot well and took

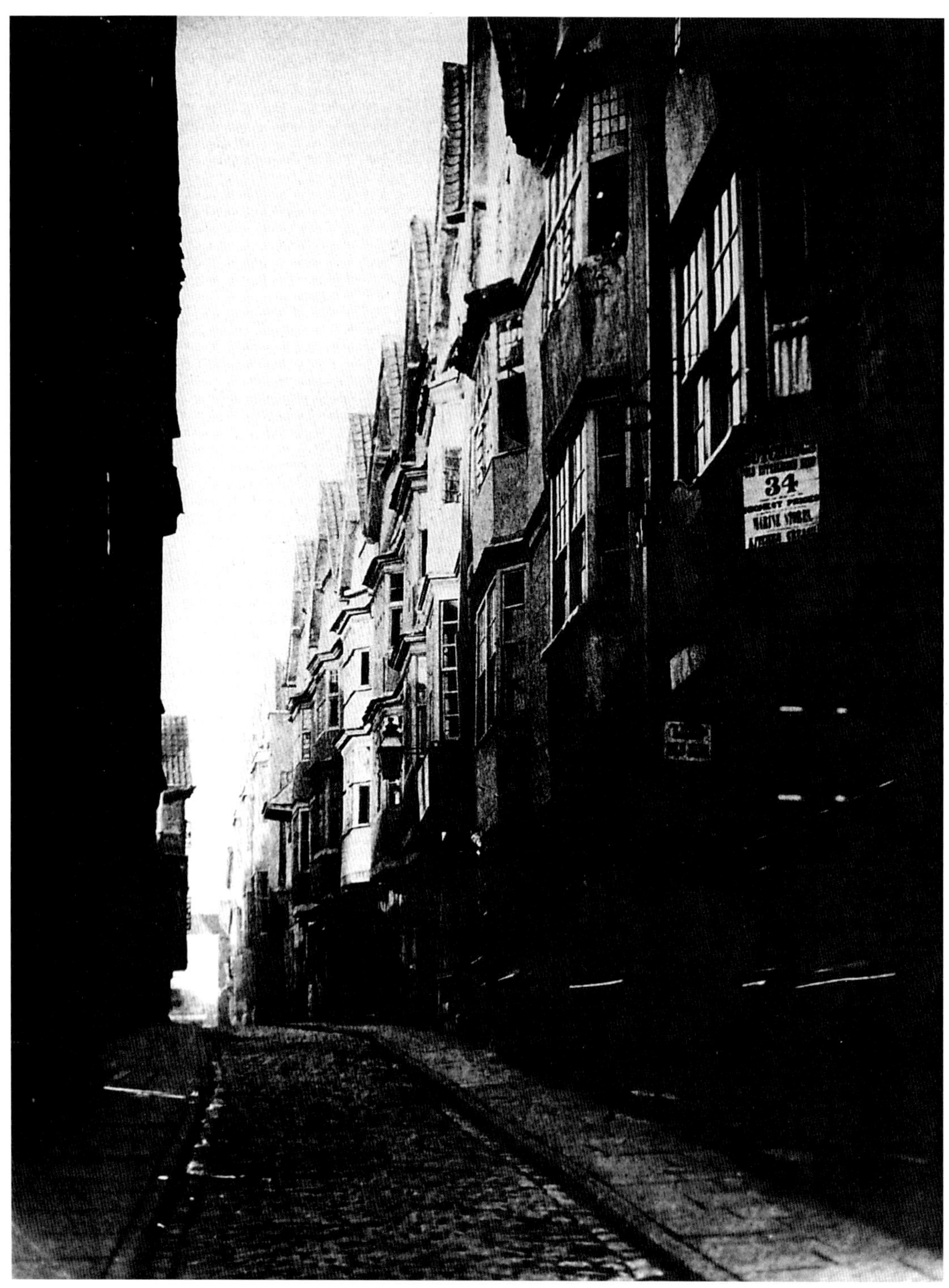

34

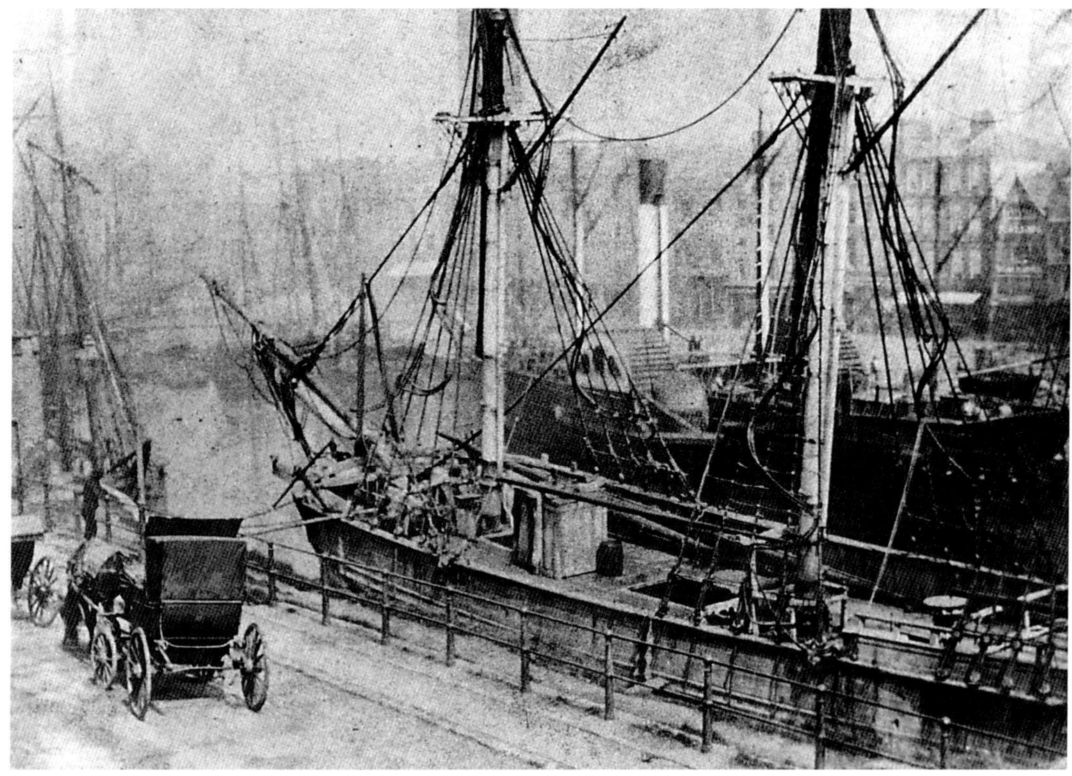

Opposite: Host Street by Hugh Owen (1808-1897). Owen's striking study of 17th century houses in Host Street was taken from the bottom of Christmas Steps. The low camera angle stresses the narrowness and gradient of the street and the rising height of the buildings. Hugh Owen was particularly skilful in his use of strong daylight to add drama to his pictures.

Photo: Bristol Records Office

Above: The steps adjacent to St Augustine's Church provided early Bristol photographers with one of their best and most popular vantage points. Numerous photographs of this section of Bristol's famous medieval harbour on the banks of the River Frome were taken in Victorian times.

The invention of photography coincided with the rapid introduction of steam-power to sea-going ships - the old traditional sailing vessel in the foreground is contrasted with a newly introduced steam-packet trading with important Irish ports such as Waterford, Cork and Dublin.

Photo: Bristol Museums and Art Gallery

an active interest in the science of photography, often discussing processes with him. Owen himself adopted the Fox Talbot Calotype method using paper negatives and very long exposures. By the mid-1840s he had become an active and successful photographer.

In 1847 Owen was one of a dozen amateurs who founded The Photographic Club - or Calotype Club - in London. Significantly, several of the 12 were artists, including the miniaturist Sir William Newton and the sculptor Frederick Scott Archer. The meetings were informal and took place in each others' homes where members could compare technical notes, swap prints and show and admire their latest pictures.

Owen's reputation was so well established within a few years that when the Great Exhibition was held in 1851, he was one of two photographers chosen to make the official record of the event held in the Crystal Palace at Hyde Park. Four commemmorative volumes of his and his colleague's photographs were presented to Queen Victoria.

Owen was at the Society of Arts headquarters in London in January 1853 when the Photographic Society - later the Royal Photographic Society - was founded. He was elected a member of the society's 21-strong Council. Significantly, he was one of at least three of the first Council members to choose the Bristol landscape as a major theme in their work. The others included Fox Talbot's friend, the Reverend Calvert R. Jones from Bath and John Dilwyn Llewelyn, who lived near Swansea. The brilliant Roger Fenton, the great photographer of the Crimean War, was elected Secretary that evening. Owen stood shoulder to shoulder with the very best.

Hugh Owen's inspirations were identical to those of the artists and poets who had preceded him. He loved things medieval and he loved the countryside surrounding Bristol. He explored the cloisters of Bristol Cathedral as well as photographing his beloved St Mary Redcliffe Church. He worked in Leigh Woods and is credited as being the very first photographer to take a picture of a cornfield. The first attempts had failed because the yellow of the corn registered as black with the early emulsions.

Owen's undoubted skills were recognised not just by his photographic peers but also by the London critics who were starting to take photography more and more seriously as an art form. He had a dozen Calotypes accepted for the first-ever Photographic Society (later the Royal Photographic Society) Annual Exhibition at the Society of British Artists gallery in Suffolk Street, Pall Mall.

These early exhibits won praise from the Royal Family, which already had copies of his Great Exhibition pictures. The critic of The Morning Post wrote: "Mr Hugh Owen, of Bristol, contributes several artistic studies of surpassing beauty, with which the Royal party were greatly pleased". Another stated: "A group from Nature, by Hugh Owen, is very wonderful."

The following year The Illustrated London News, reviewing his local and Portuguese scenes, commented: "Some specimens by Mr Hugh Owen are deserving of high commendation: we may particularise some charming views from Leigh Woods, near Bristol. There are, too, some fine views of convents and old buildings in Oporto by Mr Hugh Owen. The striking contrast of light and shade in these views is remarkable, the light entering through the open cloisters, and the dark masses of shadow beneath the rich groining of the roof are most effectively and distinctly rendered."

Shortly before he abandoned photography because of his dislike of the new processes involving the use of chemicals which he found unpleasant, Owen was once again praised to the skies for the quality of his work. He had written to the Photographic Society Journal in 1854 to defend the Fox Talbot Calotype process during a heated debate between supporters of paper negatives and those who preferred the collodion

---

Opposite: Leigh Woods in the 1850s . . . the amateur artist George Cumberland (1754-1848) wrote of a visit to Leigh Woods: "I rose at 5 o'clock and set off alone for a walk to avoid the great heats . . . I crossed the ferry, wound up the happy valley reading Dante's Paradiso, and setting down at each shady tree, it was then 7 o'clock and the rabbits ran about like tame ones." The peace and serenity of the woods were perfectly captured on the first paper negatives.

Photo: Bristol Records Office

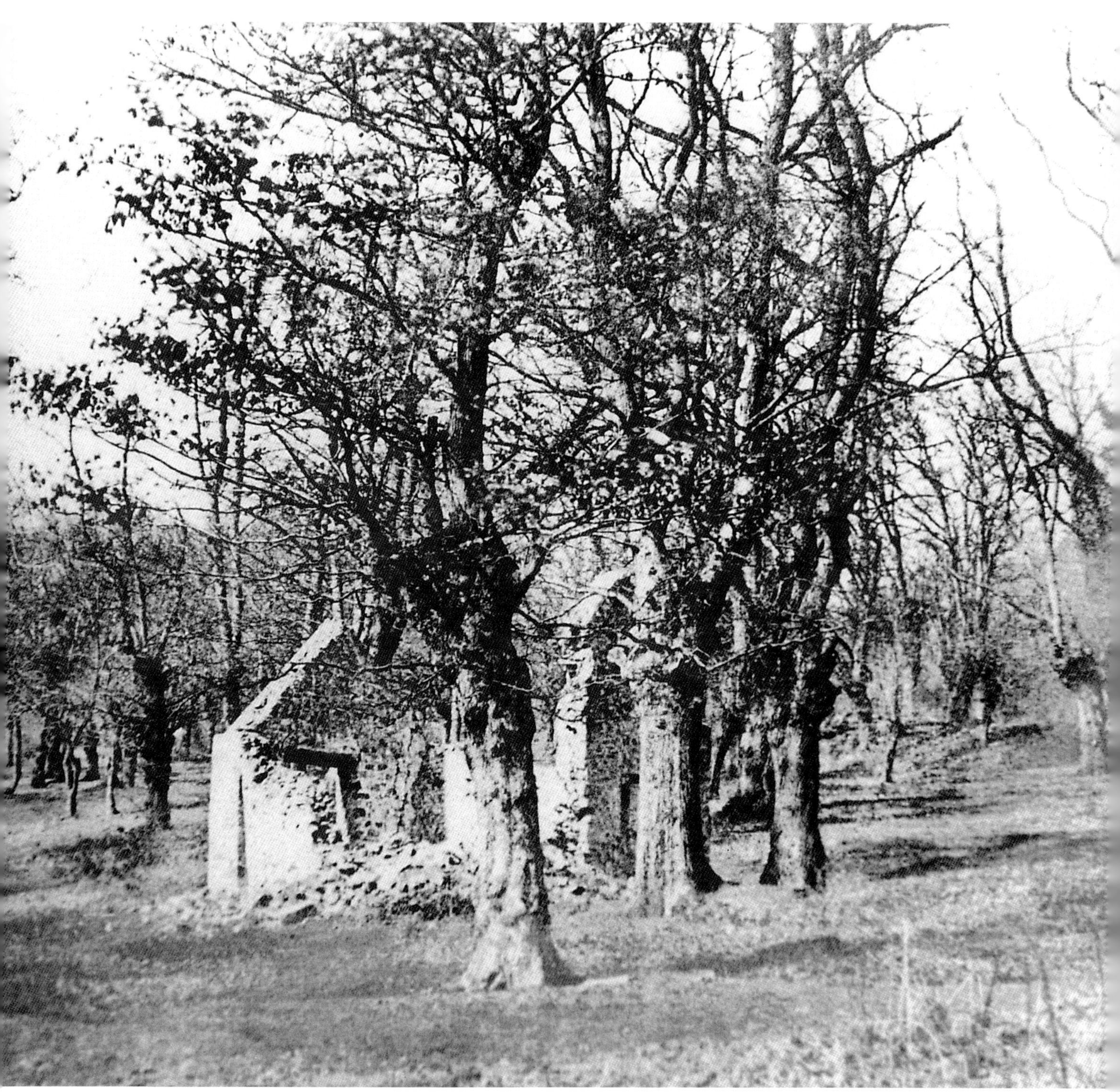

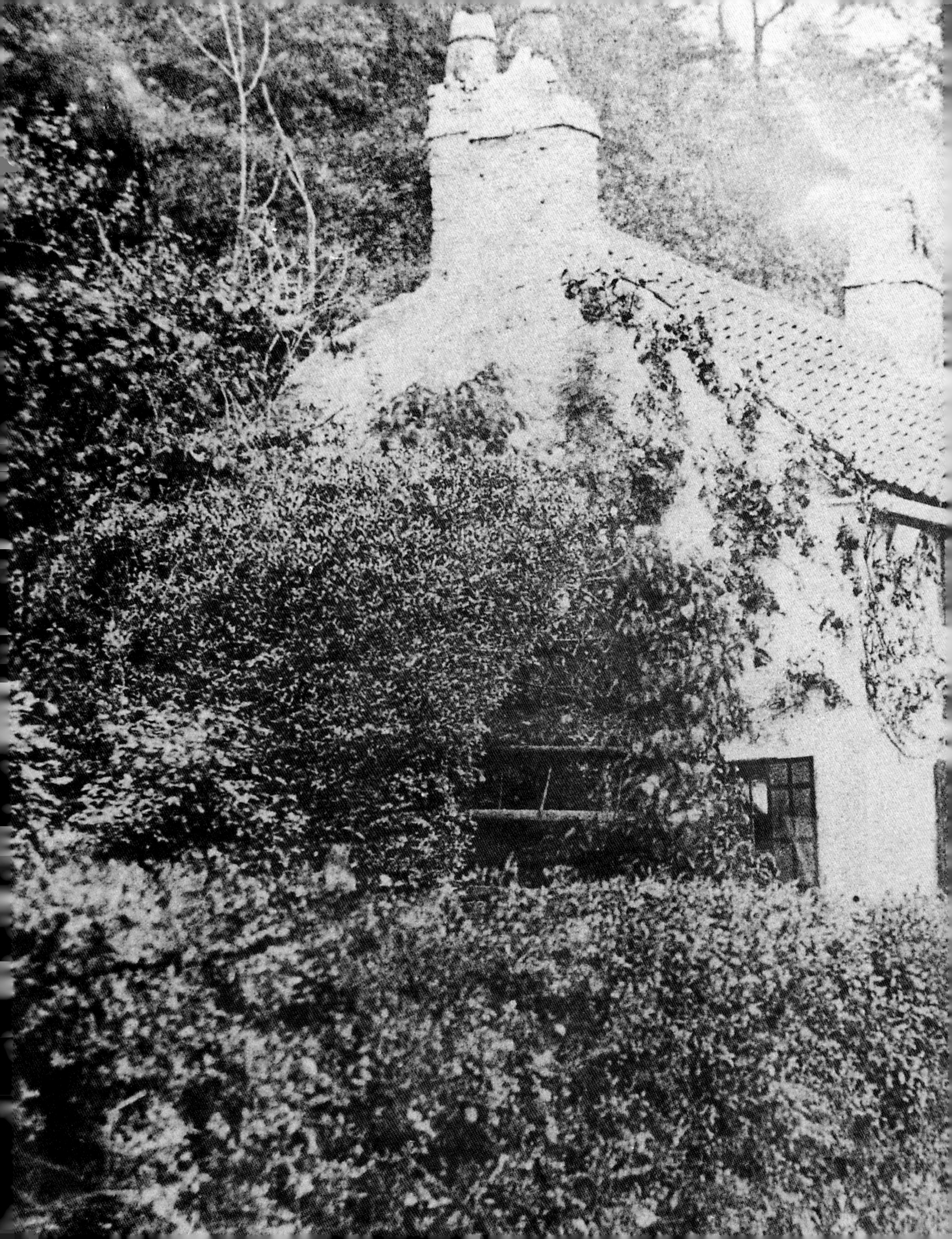

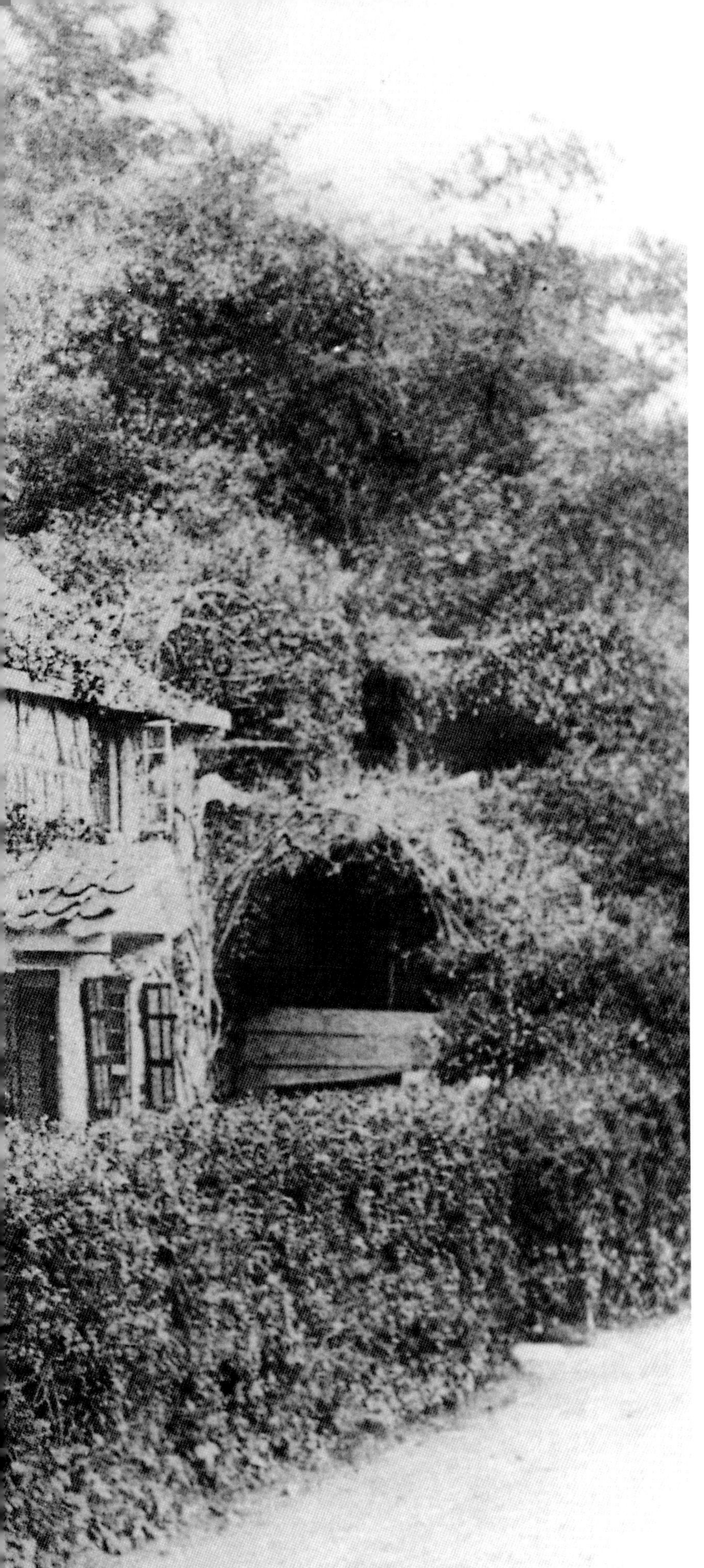

Cottage in Leigh Woods. Even before the opening of the Clifton Suspension Bridge on December 8 1864 as a belated memorial to Isambard Kingdom Brunel (1806-1859), Bristolians loved to wander in the leafy glades of Leigh Woods. This delightful, rose-clad cottage served "Tea and Coffee Every Day Except Sunday" to thirsty visitors.

Photo: Bristol Records Office

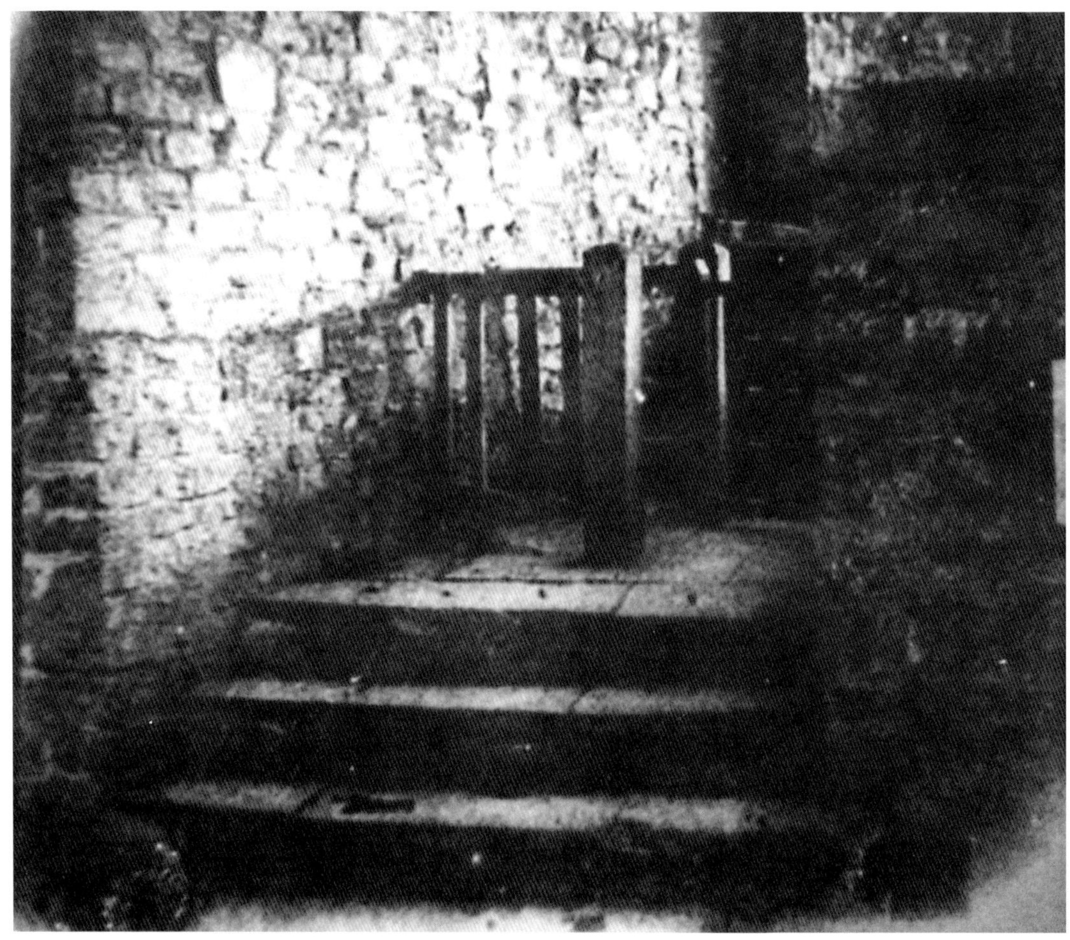

"The Wishing Gate, Redland". The photographer has carefully chosen what initially might have seemed an unprepossessing subject but, by clever use of light, given it warmth, depth and atmosphere.

Photo: Bristol Records Office

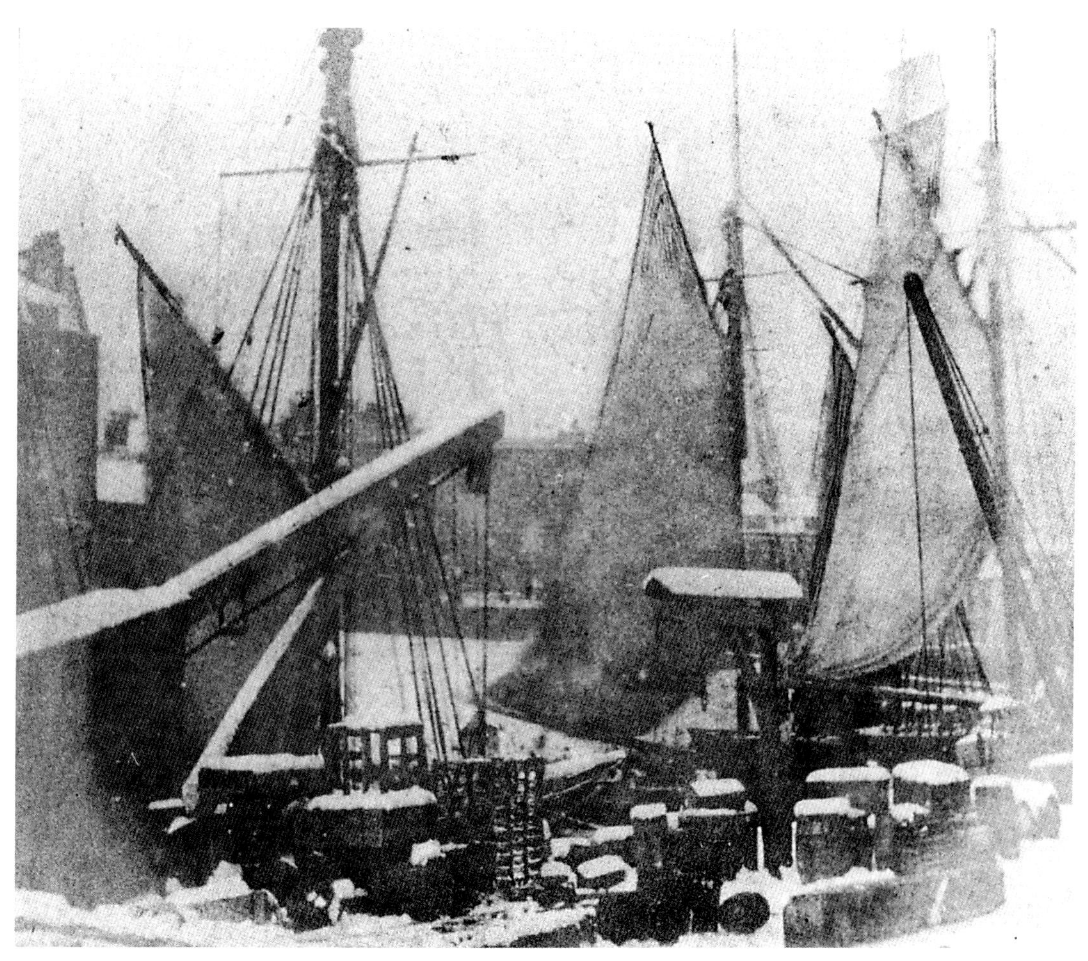

A photograph of sailing vessels and cargo at the
quayside in Bristol. This snow-covered scene - always
tricky for photographers even to the present time -
closely echoes the composition that a painter might
have used for a similar picture.

Photo: Bristol Museums and Art Gallery

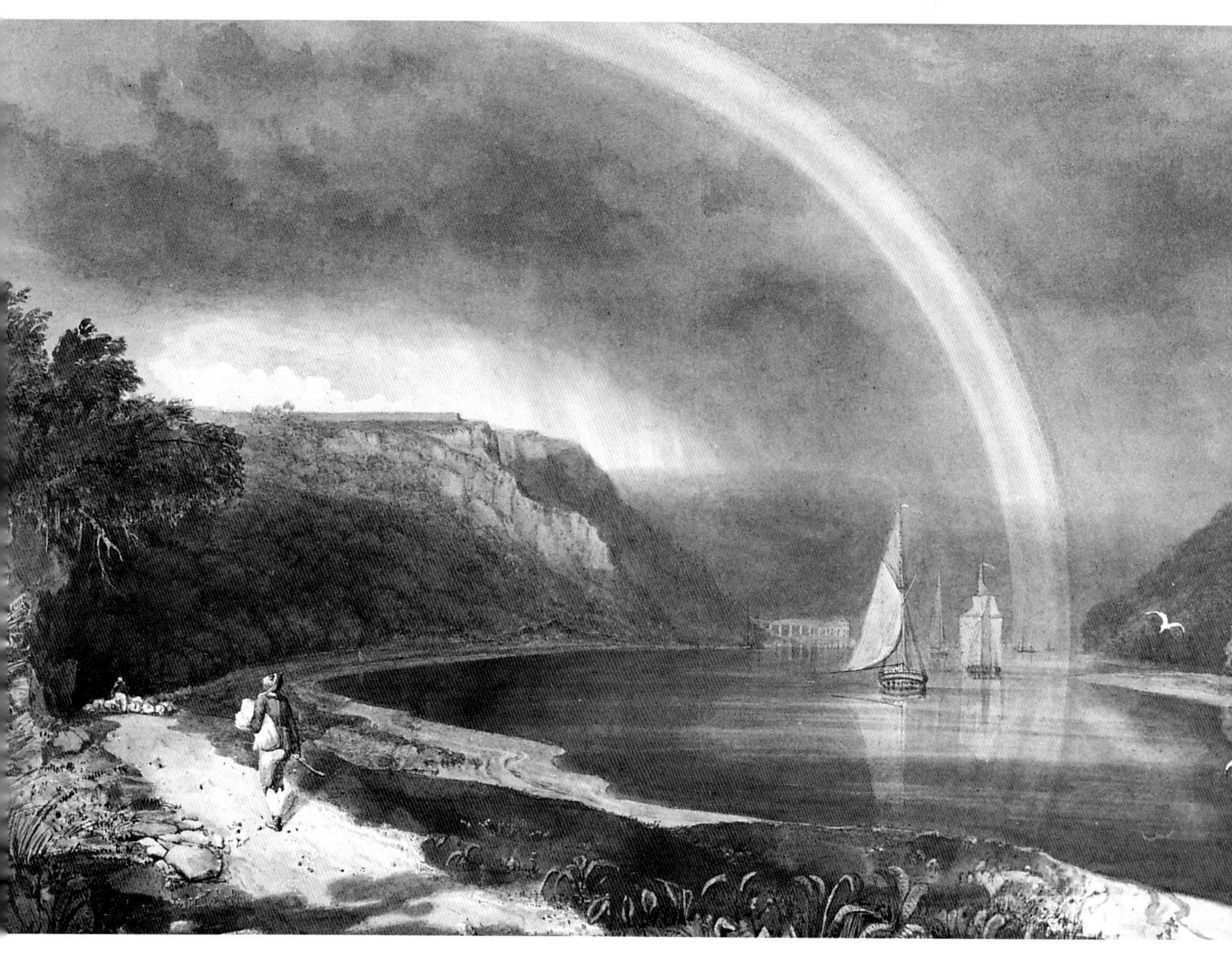

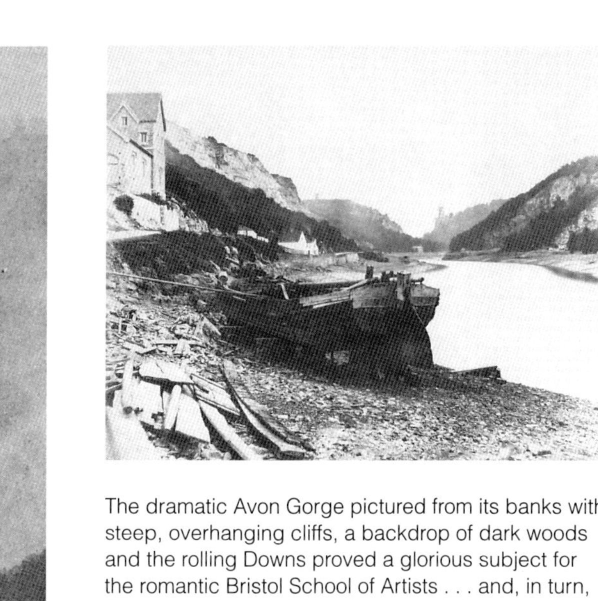

The dramatic Avon Gorge pictured from its banks with steep, overhanging cliffs, a backdrop of dark woods and the rolling Downs proved a glorious subject for the romantic Bristol School of Artists . . . and, in turn, for their photographer-followers.

Opposite: Samuel Jackson (1794-1869) painted his glowing Rainbow on the River Avon in about 1825. It shows sheep being herded along the tow-path to market in Bristol or to graze on the Downs above under breaking skies. In the distance is the group of buildings known as the New Hotwell, which enjoyed success in the mid-18th century but, being too inaccessible lost out to the rival the Hotwells Spa itself.

Above: Though Dr Brittan's photograph has the more earthbound sight of a flat-bottomed boat moored on the banks of the Avon with no arching rainbow or parting clouds yet it still manages to conjure up a strong sense of atmosphere in this brooding 1857 study of the tidal river.

Watercolour: Bristol Museums and Art Gallery; Photo: Royal Photographic Society

method. In Fox Talbot's process, paper negatives were turned into positive prints with sensitised paper while the collodion process involved wet glass plates covered with a transparent coating.

Owen argued not just for the technical opportunities that Fox Talbot's paper process offered but also for the critical control his simple method gave the photographer when making prints.

He submitted several pictures to the Journal, writing: "They are not favourable copies . . . but they have the advantage of being strictly *my own* (his italics) and produced without depending upon the assistance of photographic chemists, the use of whose advertised secret preparations renders very questionable the claims to credit of those who only pursue *the royal road* (his italics) to photography."

The Editor of the Journal was obviously won over and added:"The specimens forwarded by Mr Owen afford triumphant proofs of the perfection to which the paper process may be brought in skilful hands. They are all beautiful pictures from an artistic point of view. Mr Owen will doubtless exhibit at the approaching Exhibition and we think his 'Well on the Beach' will hardly be surpassed by anything in collodion."

Owen was one of a small band of photographers working in Bristol in the late 1840s and 1850s. Just like the Bristol School of Artists, the early photographers thoroughly enjoyed each other's company and inspiration and often went on photographic sorties together echoing the artists' sketching parties.

His great friend John Bevan Hazard (died 1892) was another leading light and the two often photographed together during the early 1850s, both clearly inspired by the familiar Bristol sights - the Gorge, the woodlands, old Bristol. Other colleagues were Dr Brittan who took fine pictures of identical scenes and Owen's fellow Photographic Society Council members, the Reverend Calvert R. Jones from Bath and John Dilwyn Llewelyn from South Wales.

Documented information about many of these early photographers is maddeningly elusive, vague and fragmentary. Very little research has been done and even the Royal Photographic Society itself can only offer a paragraph or two about Hugh Owen and almost none on other early Bristol photographers. Reece Winstone, the well-known Bristol photographer, collector and publisher of old Bristol photographs, recognised Owen's talents and did what research he could, tracking down some of his descendants and positively identifying his pictures from a collection presented to him.

In later life Owen went on to devote his spare time and his considerable talents to a study of the history of Bristol Pottery (there is a

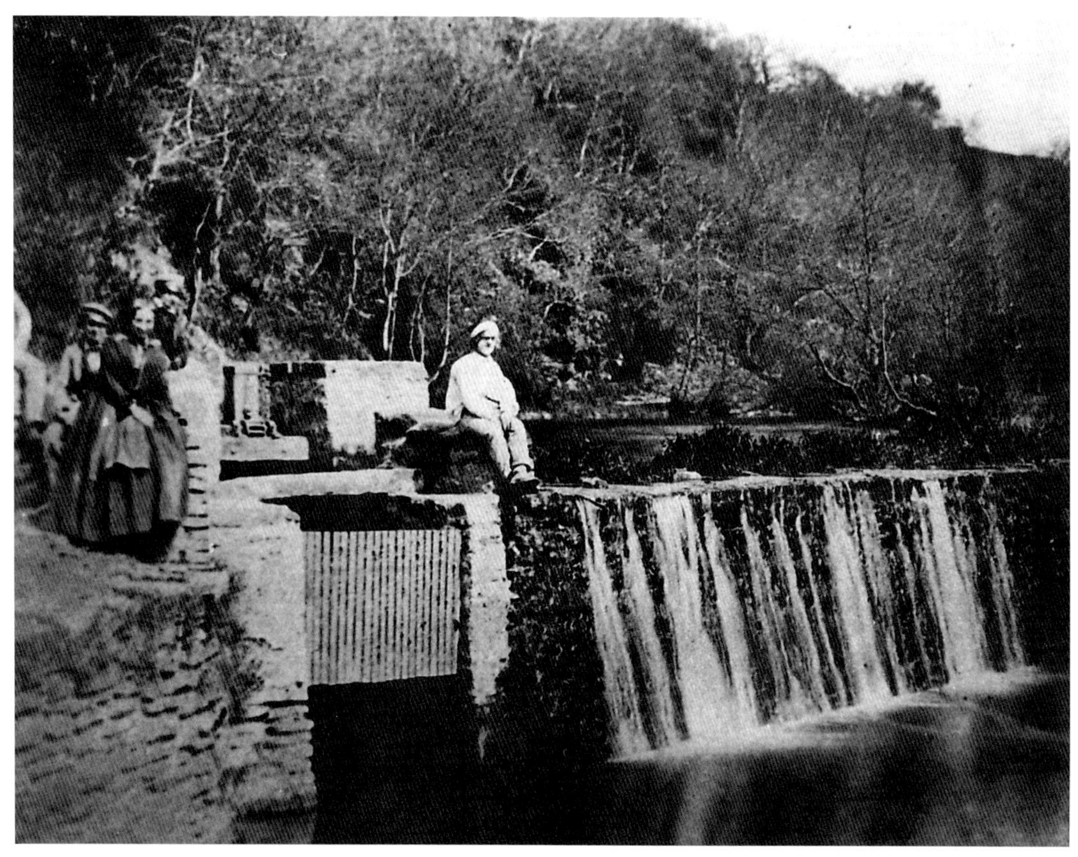

Stapleton Glen in the 1850s and a group of figures by
Snuff Mill weir are frozen into immobility for the long
seconds the picture would have required.

Photo, Bristol Records Office

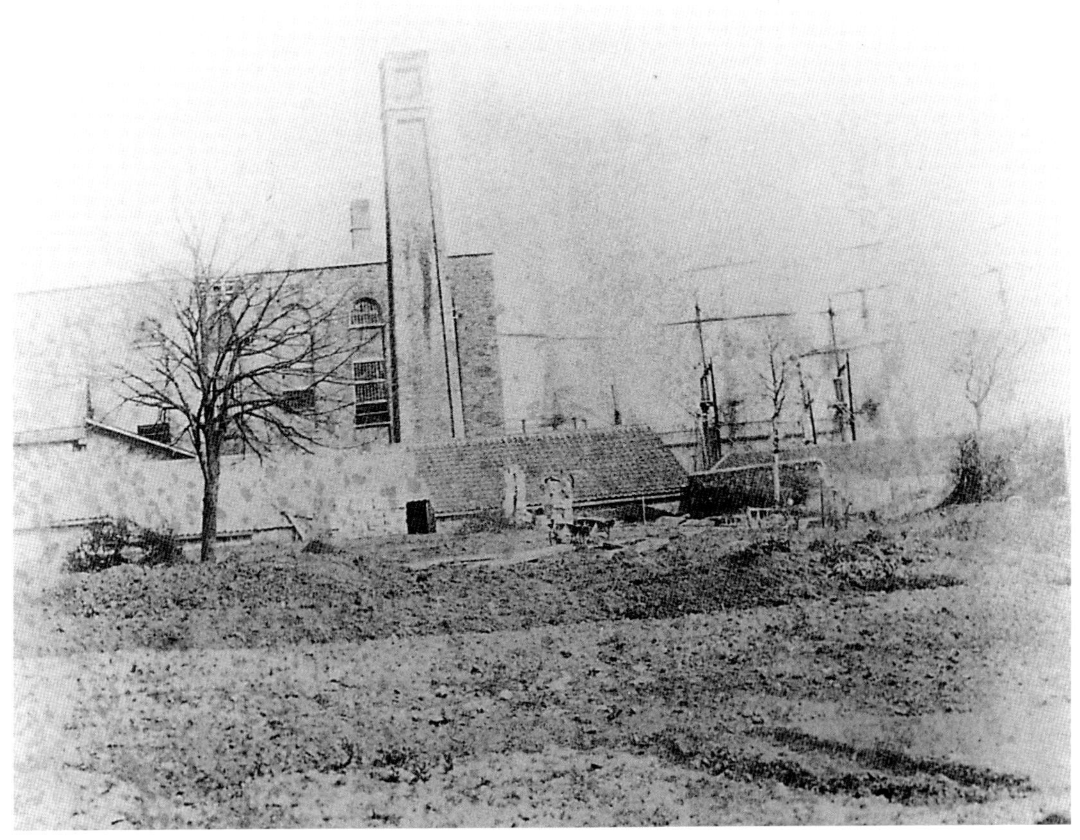

Wapping Wharf and a typical dockside skyline in old Bristol with a harbour which continued to be dominated by the tall masts of ocean-going trading ships despite its loss of trade to younger, more easily approached ports like Liverpool.

Photo: Bristol Records Office

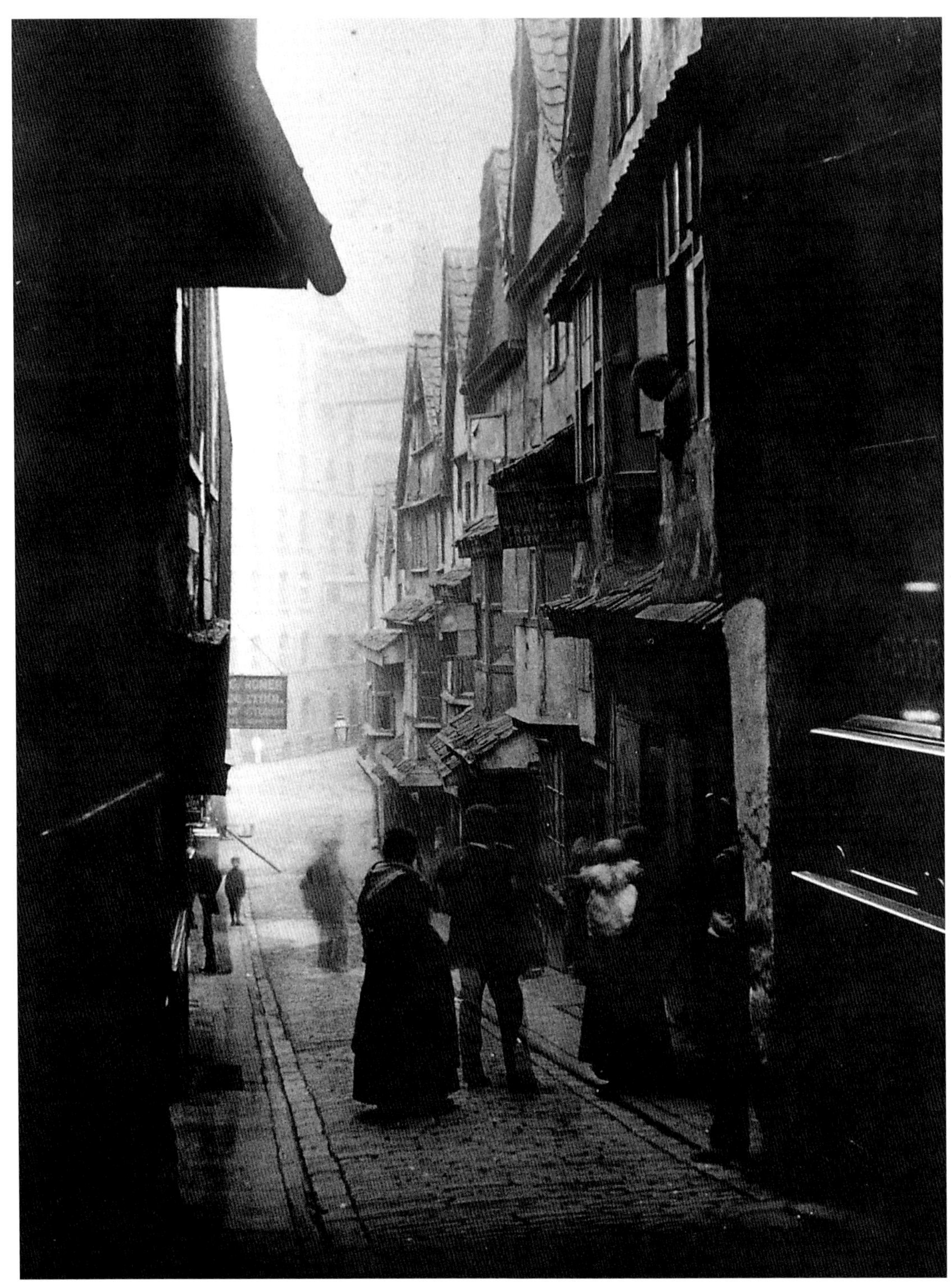

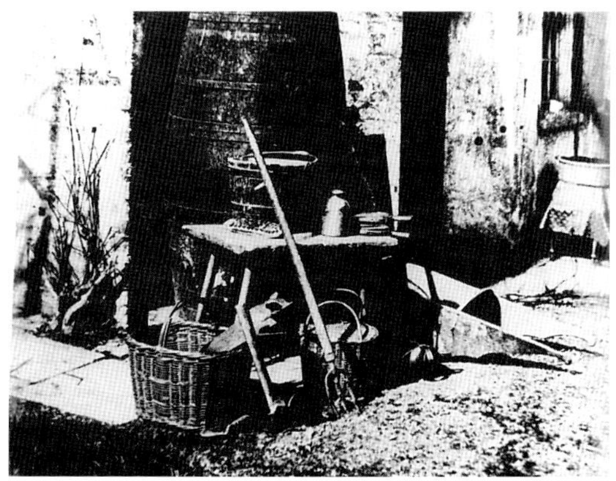

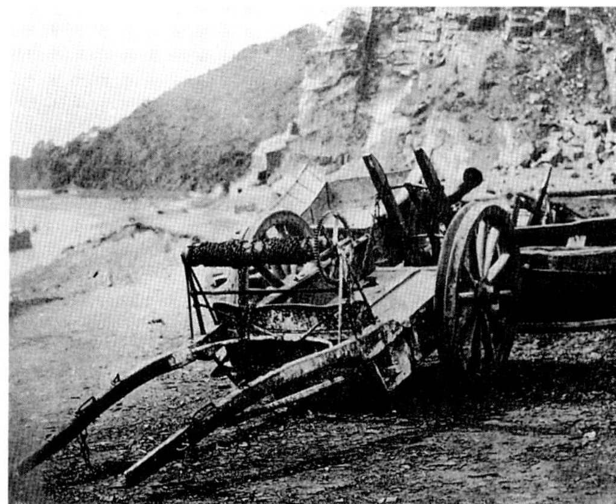

Above: Black Rock by John Bevan Hazard (died 1892) is a more than dispassionate observation of this heavy-duty cart with its hand-operated winch used to load and transport large blocks of stone quarried in the Sea Walls area. The thoughtful, balanced composition and fine detailing make this picture much more than a factual record of an interesting item of industrial equipment.

Photo: Bristol Records Office

Opposite: Bristol's narrow, high-sided streets near the city centre were a continuing source of fascination for early photographers long after the pioneering days of Hugh Owen (1808-1897) and John Bevan Hazard (died 1892). Here light is used artfully to capture the bustle of inner city life in a turn-of-the-century picture.

Photo: Bristol Museums and Art Gallery

Left: Photography was in its infancy when another important theme in painting - the still life - was hijacked and re-worked by the first cameramen. Some of their efforts were over-elaborate and self-conscious but this cluttered arrangement of simple garden tools amid a wide range of surfaces and shapes works admirably.

Photo: Bristol Records Office

---

comprehensive collection in the City Museum and Art Gallery) which was published as a book in 1873.

By then the best of the old pictures had been taken, not only in Bristol - John Hazard appears to have abandoned photography not long after Owen - but also in London and, notably, Edinburgh where the Scottish painter David Octavius Hill produced a treasure trove of Calotypes in the 1840s widely regarded as some of the finest-ever examples of photographic art.

The high-mindedness and enthusiastic experimentation of the early practitioners of the 1840s and 1850s who strove for artistry above all was becoming diluted. Photography was turning into a widespread commercial enterprise and was no longer the exclusive territory of an elite of well-off, gifted amateurs.

The pioneers, burdened in the field by cumbersome equipment, had had to take extreme care in composing their long-exposure studies and the darkroom processes involved in developing and editing were equally painstaking. Improved technology and lighter, more reliable cameras made the taking of a picture far less of a business - and far cheaper too.

Now reportage, current affairs, ceremonial events and everyday street scenes had become standard fare. Long before the end of the century, the introduction of the roll film transformed photography into a hugely popular hobby which millions could enjoy with never a thought of the noble ideals of its founders.

But the photographer as artist remained the guiding light.

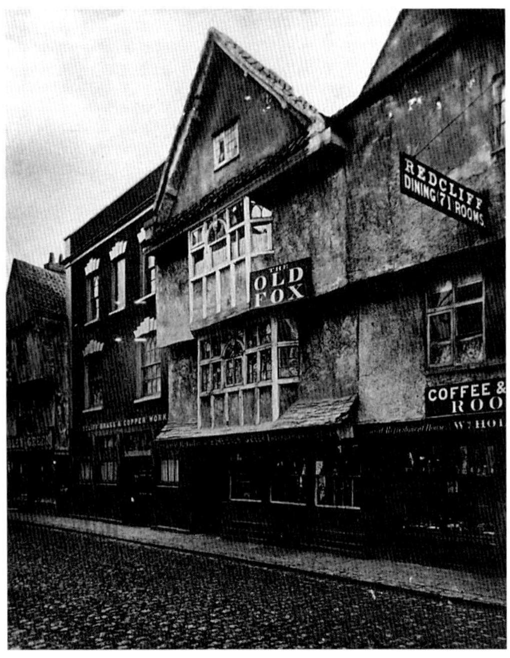

Above: The bay-fronted, steep gabled Old Fox in Redcliffe with, to the left, the famous Redcliff brass and copper works and, to the right, the Redcliff dining rooms . . . typical town buildings in Victorian Bristol.

Photo: Bristol Museums and Art Gallery

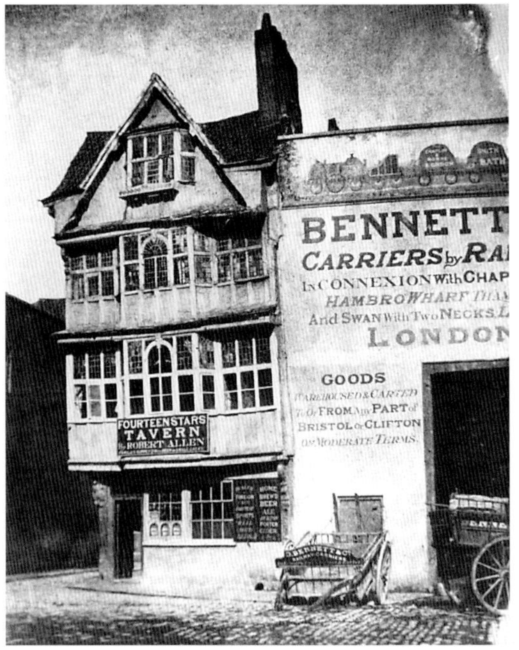

Above: The Fourteen Stars by Hugh Owen (1808-1897). This picture of the 17th century tavern in Counterslip with its adjoining goods carriers depot, is one of Owen's early architectural studies. A lost corner of Bristol . . . the inn was demolished in 1857.

Photo: Bristol Records Office

Opposite: News events like the heavy flooding in central Bristol in 1889 became standard fare for the later Victorian photographers, as this vivid study of Old King Street at the height of the floods shows so clearly. In the foreground, two men in a horse-drawn carriage look back at crowds surveying the floods. The use of foreground figures was taken directly from art.

Photo: Bristol Museums and Art Gallery

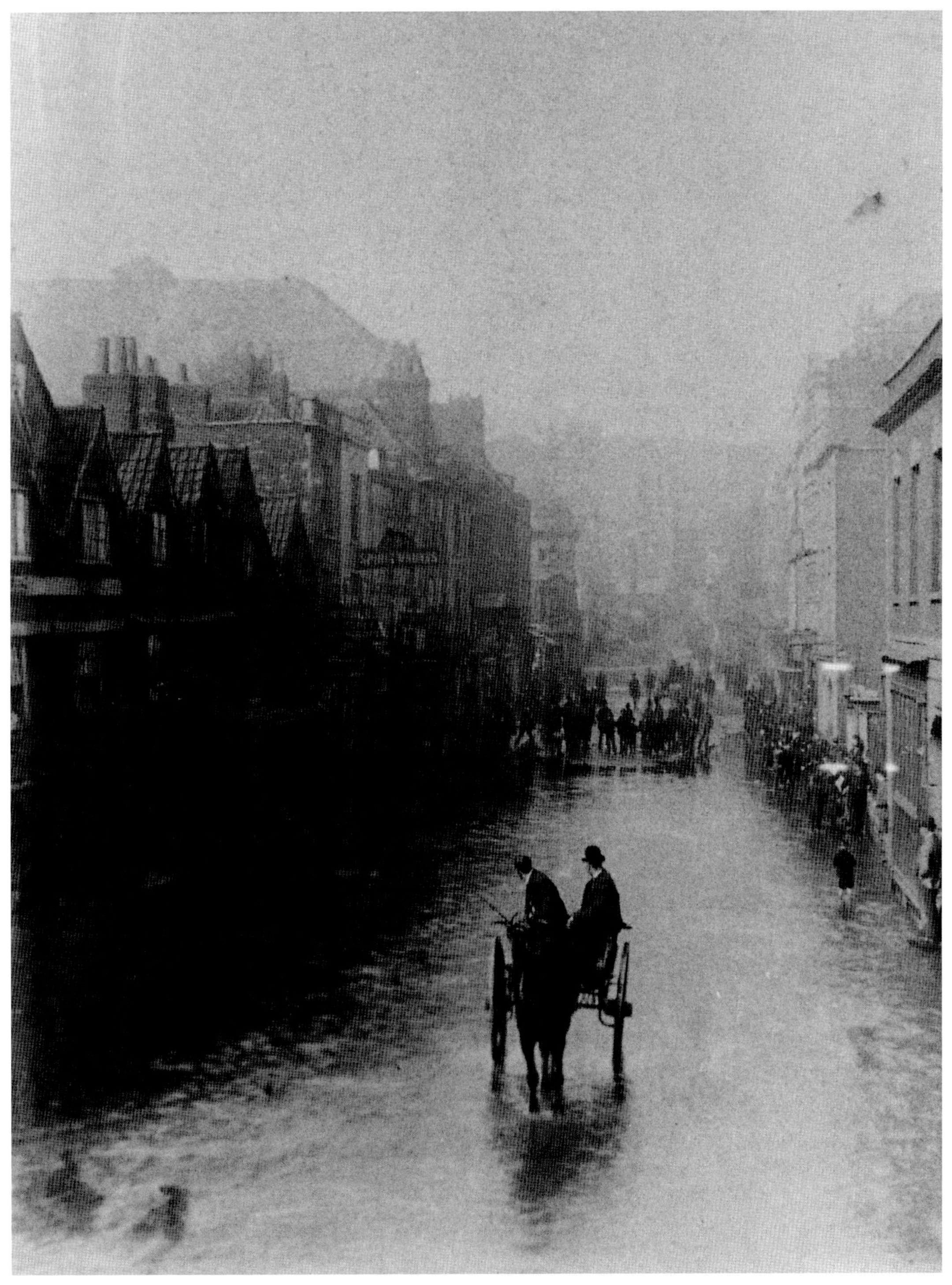

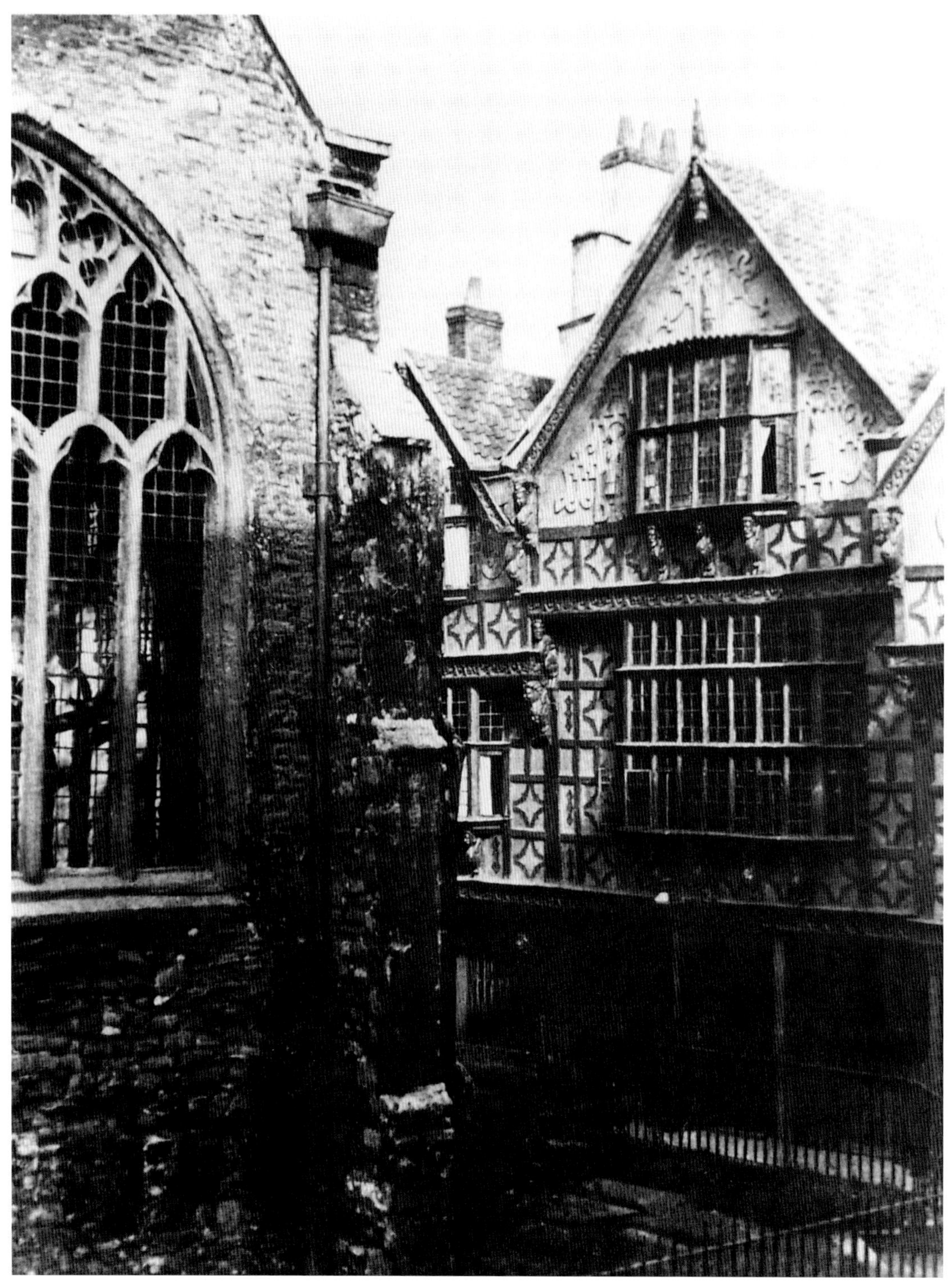

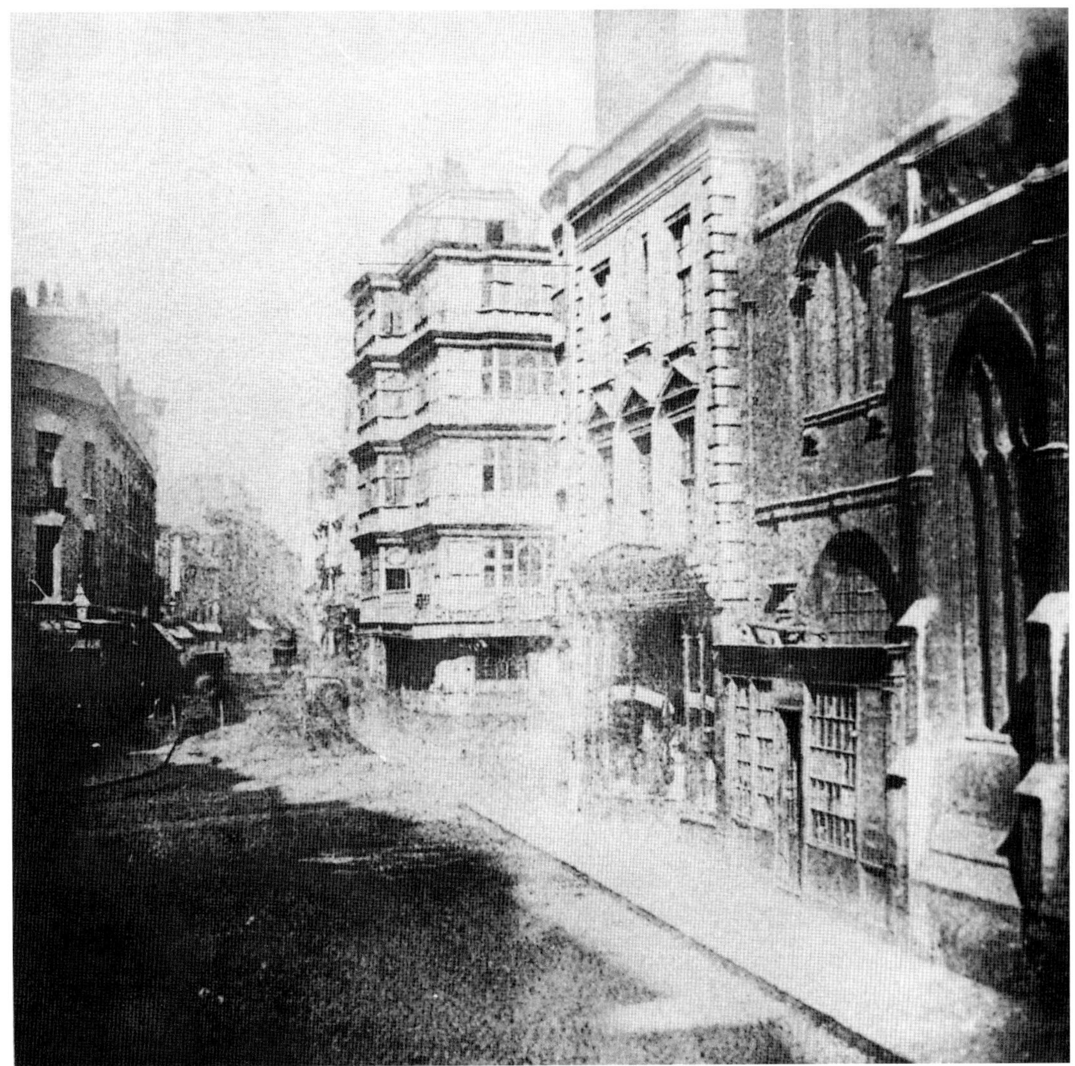

Above: The Dutch House, on the corner of High Street and Wine Street, attracted early photographers not just from Bristol but from other parts of the country. They were thrilled by the camera's ability to capture all the details of such an extraordinarily elaborate street facade - except the passers-by, of course.

The Dutch House was one of the saddest losses of the first major air raid on central Bristol on Sunday November 24, 1940. It was badly damaged and, in the impetuous clear-up which followed the raid, its still-standing structure was quickly pulled down.

Photo: Bristol Museums and Art Gallery

Opposite: St Peter's Hospital. Hugh Owen (1808-1897) at his most creative. Despite a very awkward camera position, he manages to create a fine composition which highlights the character of this beautiful building.

St Peter's Hospital and much of the surrounding area was lost in the first great Bristol Blitz on Sunday November 24, 1940. Its roof melted into a silver river of molten lead.

Photo: Bristol Records Office

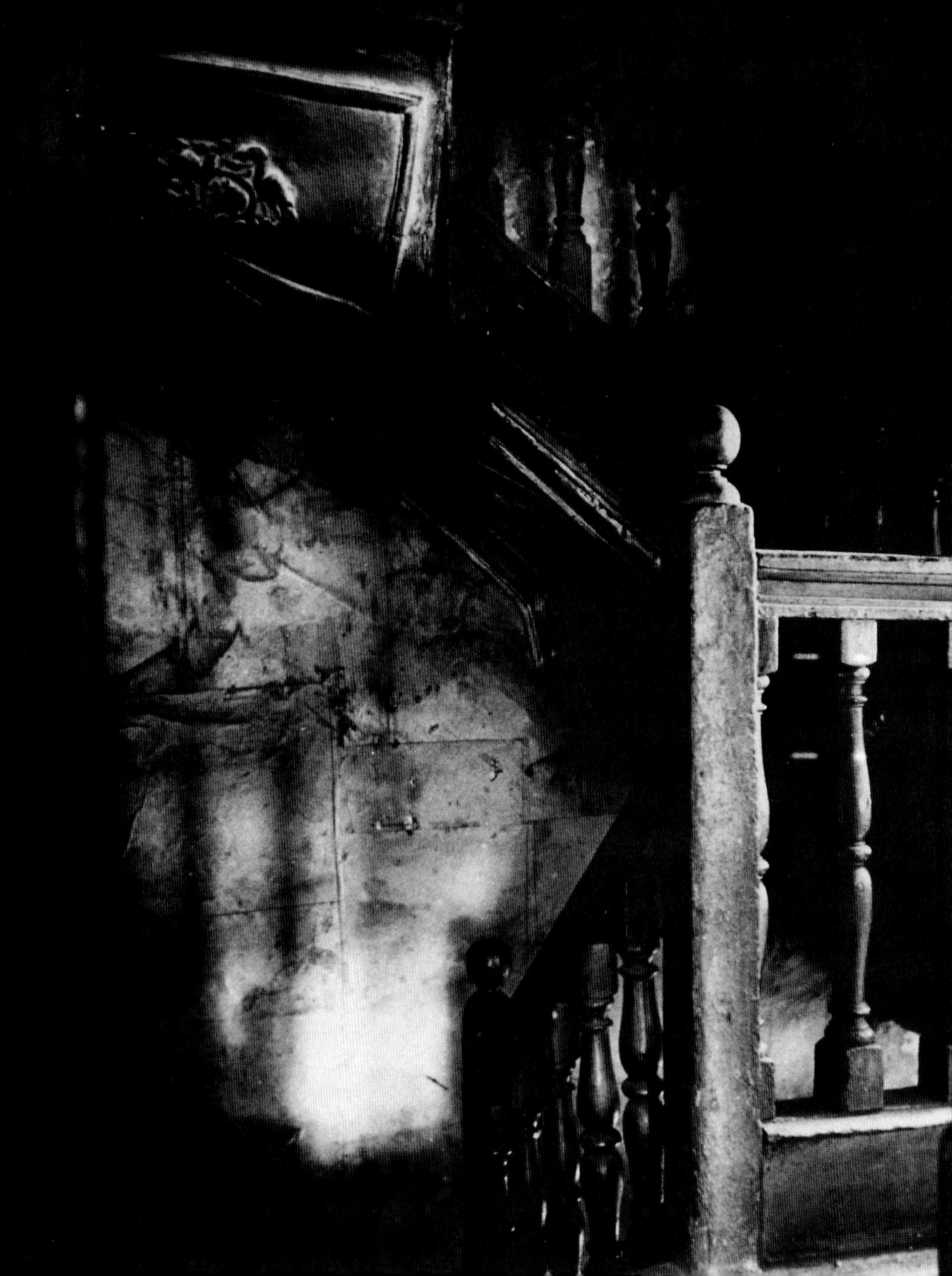

Art versus Photography

". . . a noble invention . . ." John Ruskin

". . . I am glad I have had my day" J.M.W. Turner

In January 1839 the great British chemist and physicist Michael Faraday rose before an audience at the Royal Institution in London to announce two remarkable photographic discoveries. One was the Daguerreotype from France. The other was the Calotype, invented by William Henry Fox Talbot from Lacock in Wiltshire.

Faraday exhibited examples of both types of photograph and told his listeners: "No human hand has hitherto traced such lines as these drawings display. Nature has become man's drawing-mistress."

Faraday described the pictures as the products of an important new system of "Photogenic drawing" . . . which is what pure scientists felt both Daguerre and Fox Talbot had stumbled across in their different ways. It was just another mechanical way of drawing - if a very good one -

and Faraday's lecture created little fuss or excitement.

Six months later, when photography was first patented at the Academy of Sciences in Paris, the painter Paul Delaroche - whose art students included Hugh Owen's colleague Roger Fenton - examined some photographs and roundly declared: "From this day on, painting is dead."

By the 1840s, as techniques improved, some were brazenly claiming the best results were starting to equal the drawings of Rembrandt, Sir Joshua Reynolds and Constable. And when the earliest, blurred, shadowy images gave way to full-blooded photographic portraits, landscapes and townscapes, all bright with details beyond the representational skill of any artist, the full potential - and implications - began to be appreciated.

It is not difficult to imagine the wonder the pictures caused since a century-and-a-half later the process still has the power to fascinate us. Anyone who watches a piece of blank white paper floating in a tray of chemicals gradually become a recognisable picture in a photographic studio knows the feeling. At first nothing happens. Then, like a flame creeping across paper, shadows start

---

Opposite: A beautiful interior shot of an unknown but clearly ancient building with the light casting a glow on the woodwork of the staircase and its balusters.

Photo: Bristol Records Office

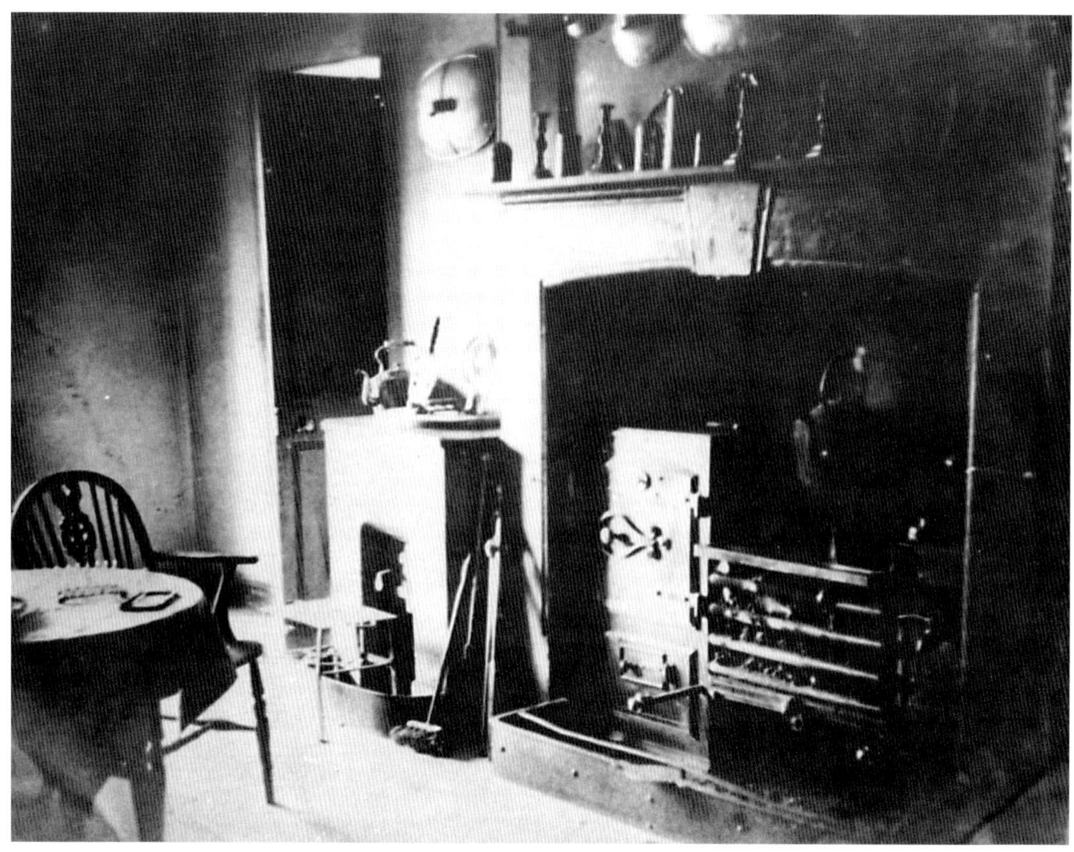

Above: A detail of the kitchen at the Fedden's home in Redland, which perfectly illustrates the early photographers' love affair with the effect of light illuminating different surfaces, wood, metal, iron and masonry.

Photo: Bristol Records Office

Opposite: Hugh Owen (1808-1897) took immense care to light this picture of a nude statue as artfully as possible. Early photographic nudes tended to be of statues . . . it was only later that photographers began to venture into the world of the Life Class and make the nude and the erotic two of photography's major themes.

Photo: Bristol Museums and Art Gallery

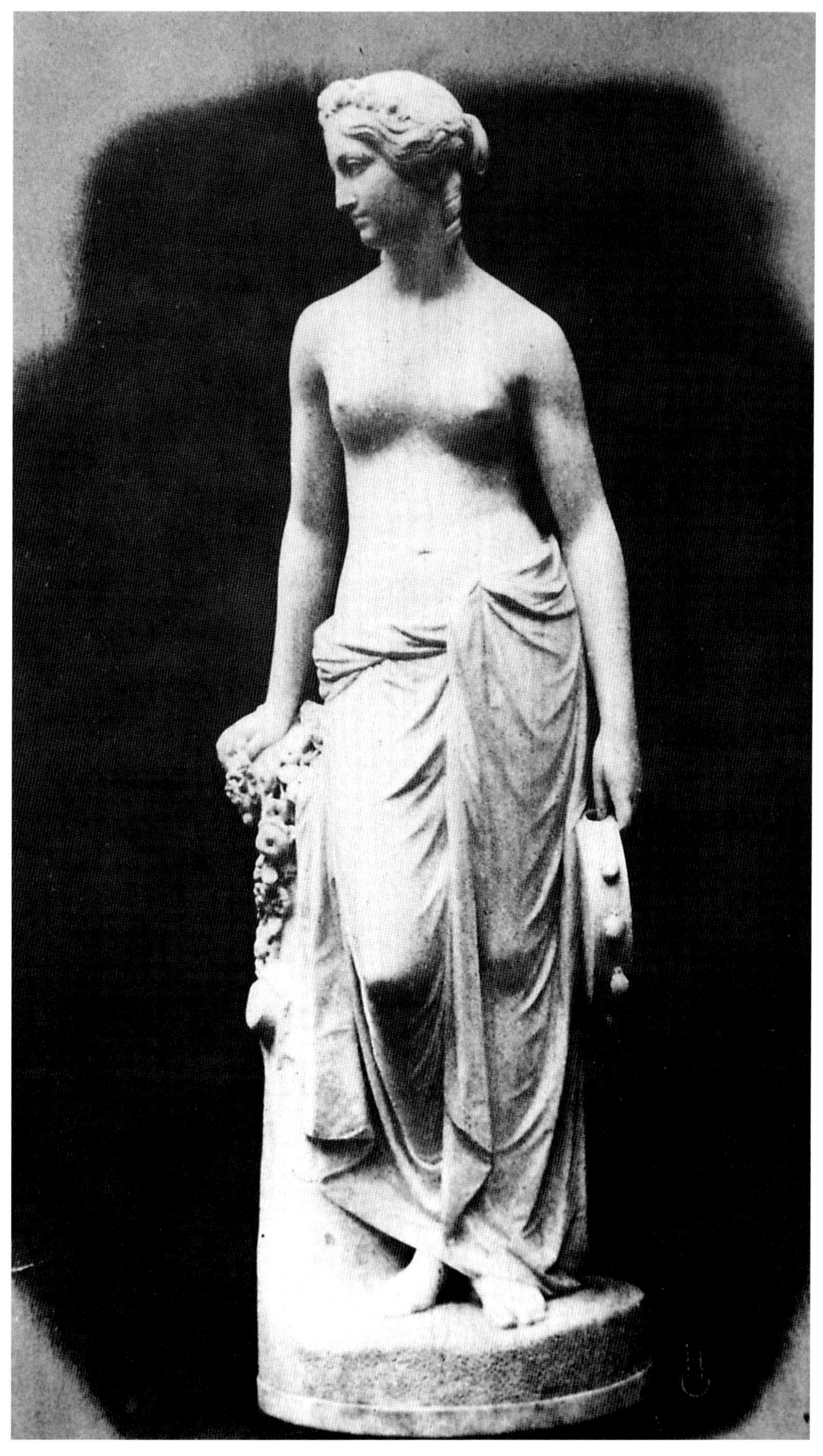

to appear, to merge and, as if by magic, form a clear image. No matter how many times you witness the process, it always has a mystical quality.

By the 1850s the debate was hotting up. Reviewers were fulsome in their praise of this innovative new art form. Some artists, particularly jobbing ones who made a living from portraiture and illustration, recognised the threat and did their Luddite best to strangle the newcomer at birth. All in vain.

As for the first photogaphers, they saw themselves as practitioners of the art of the future and promptly tried to hijack, with varying degrees of success, every painterly subject their cameras could film.

Children were posed in "artistic" groups as cherubs. Pretty girls were dressed as angels and madonnas. The dignity of labourers and snobbery of the rising middle classes was objectively caught. Still lifes were artfully assembled and frozen on film in imitation of the Old Masters while the dramatic landscapes and classical townscapes which had previously inspired painters and writers were paraded for the would-be traveller or dreamer. In Edinburgh David Octavius Hill, using Calotypes, produced a series of superb studies which could stand alongside the very best painted portraits.

The aesthete and great arbiter of Victorian taste, the writer, critic and artist John Ruskin was an early champion. In 1845 he awarded it his seal of approval proclaiming: "Photography is a noble invention, say what they will of it. Anyone who has worked, blundered and stammered as I have done for four days and then sees the thing he has been trying to do so long in vain done perfectly and faultlessly in half a minute, won't abuse it afterwards."

Others were distinctly chilly. When Turner first saw some photographs he despairingly remarked: "I am glad I have had my day."

The converted joined the stampede and voted with their feet by abandoning paint and canvas for the instant results of Calotypes and the freedom of a new profession. Defectors included Fox Talbot himself, the art school-trained Roger Fenton and Lewis Carroll of Alice In Wonderland fame. The Pre-Raphaelite painter Ford Madox Brown had a lucrative sideline in touching up enlargements.

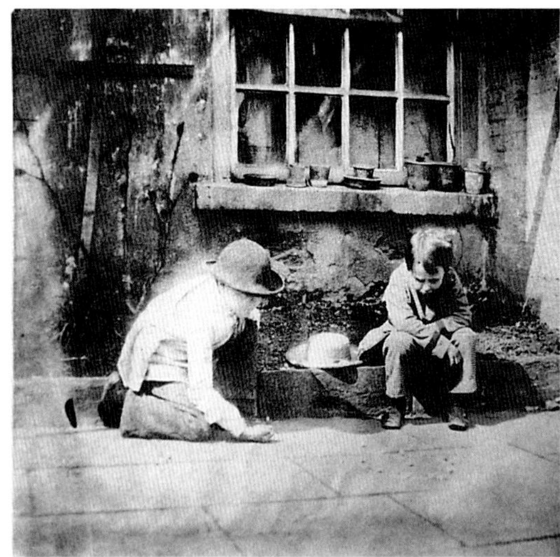

Above: This charming early 1850s photograph of two boys playing marbles by John Bevan Hazard (died 1892) captures the same sense of the timelessness and absorption of the child's world. The skill of the photographer was to make the moment seem plausible, even though the boys must have been posed. The picture is from the Fedden family album and is one of a series of intimate studies of children and adults at work, relaxing and at play.

Photo: Bristol Records Office

Right: Boys Sailing A Little Boat c. 1822 by Francis Danby (1793-1861), set in the Frome valley near Bristol and painted at a time when Danby was the father of several young children of his own.

Pictures of children at play have been an enduring subject throughout the history of art and the early photographers were as keen to record the young generation, despite the problems of exhorting children not to fidget during the long exposure times.

Painting: Bristol Museums and Art Gallery

This book's title - and the title of the exhibition it accompanies - is taken from a ringing and remarkably astute challenge made by the RPS Journal in February 1857 on photography's claim to a piece of Art's high ground.

"Photography is an enormous stride forward in the region of art. The old world is well nigh exhausted with its wearisome mothers and

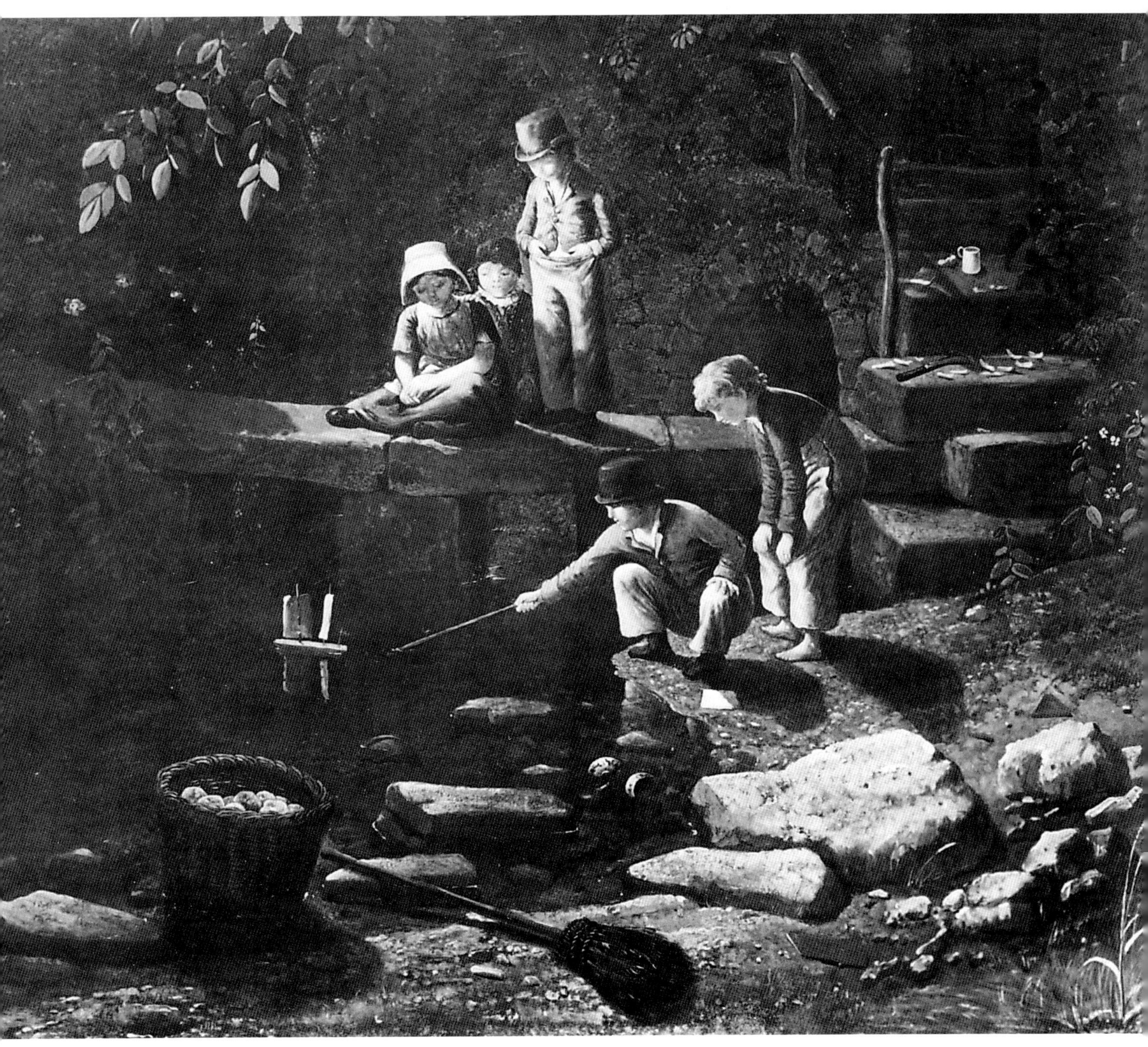

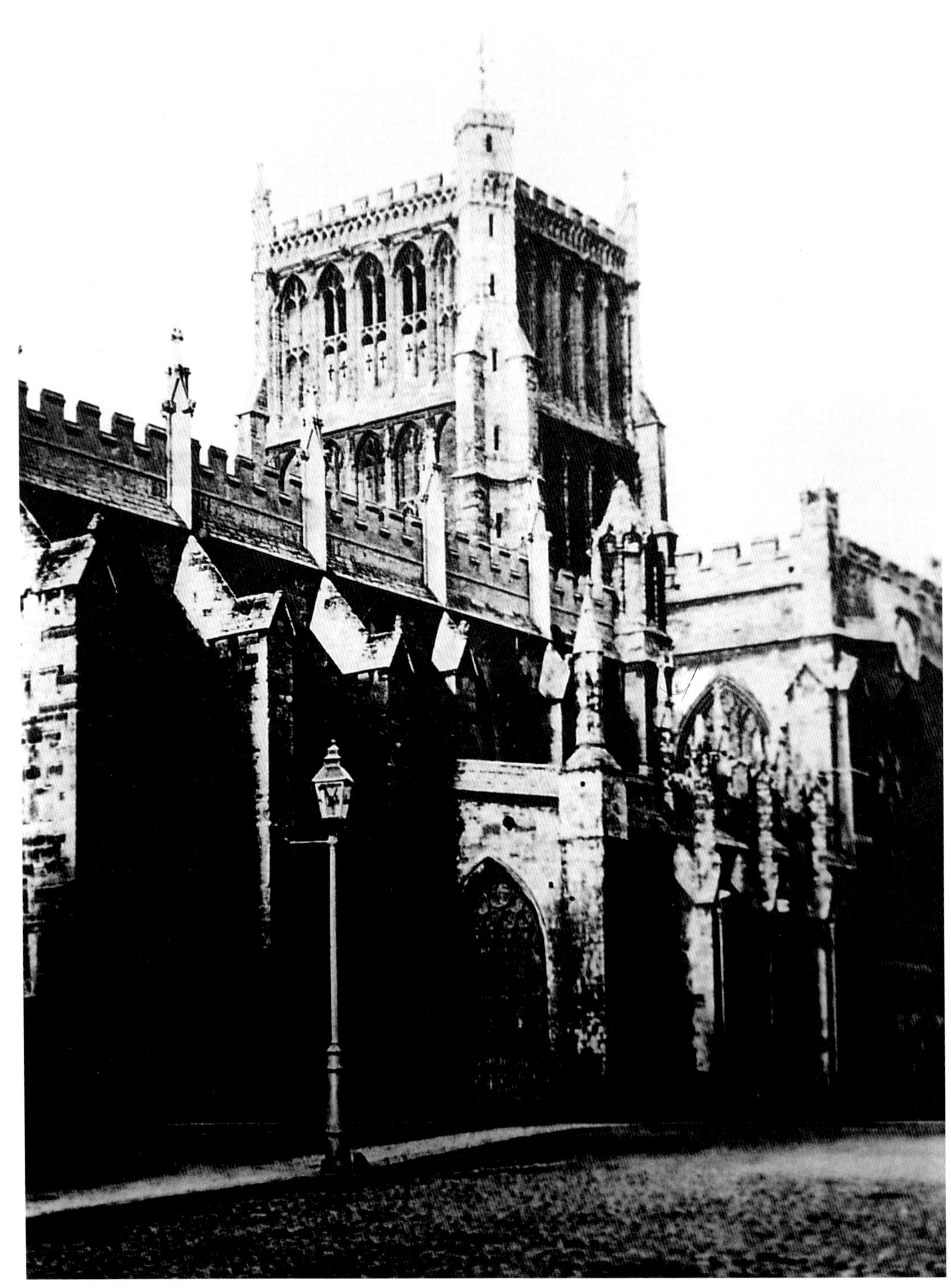

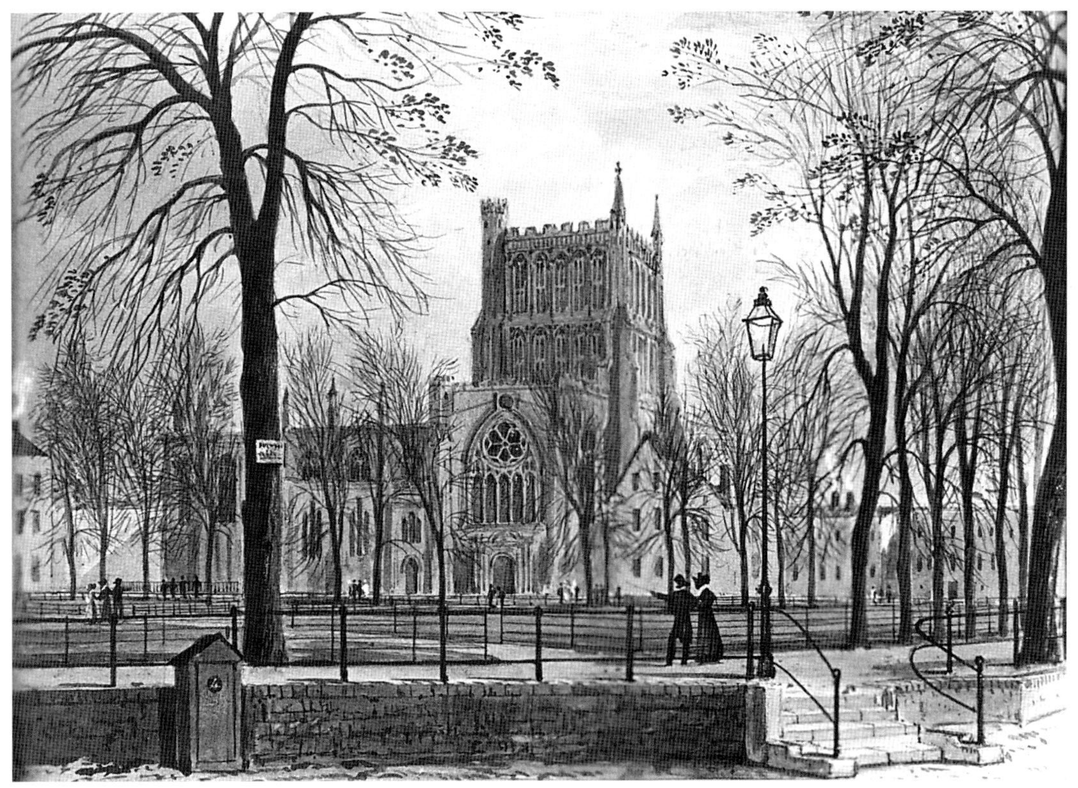

Above: College Green and Bristol Cathedral April 1827 by T.L.S. Rowbotham (1783-1856).

Bristol Cathedral, College Green and the rugged Norman arch on College Square were rich subjects for painters. T.L.S. Rowbotham's 1827 watercolour of the cathedral has a calm elegance.

Opposite: Bristol Cathedral by John Bevan Hazard (died 1892), by contrast, shows a very different scene. Hazard deliberately stresses the mass and handsome gothic decoration of the cathedral as pictured from College Green.

Watercolour: Bristol Museums and Art Gallery
Photo: Bristol Records Office

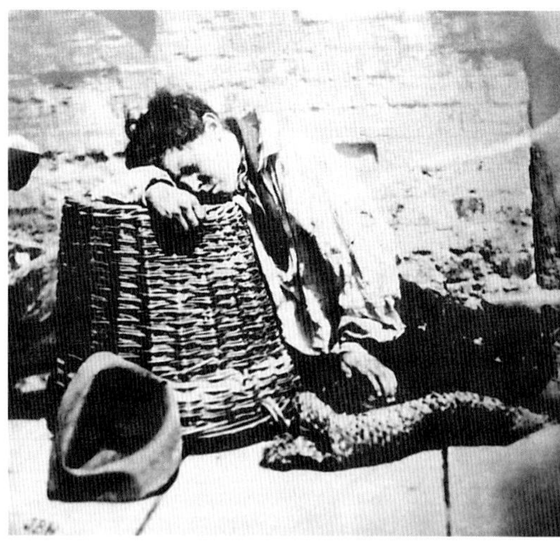

The Sleeping Boy by John Bevan Hazard (died 1892).
Part of his portfolio of intimate studies of people which
were clearly heavily influenced by the Genre paintings
- scenes of everyday life - so popular with a
sentimental Victorian public obsessed with preserving
the ideal of the family.

Photo: Bristol Records Office

children called Madonnas; its everlasting dead
bodies called Entombments; its wearisome
nudities called Nymphs and Venuses .

Then all at once breaks a small light in the far
West, a new world slowly widens to our sight . . .
This new land is Photography, Art's youngest and
fairest child; no rival of the old family, no
struggler for worn-out birthrights, but heir to a
new heaven and a new earth, found by itself and
to be left to its own children.

For photography there are new secrets to
conquer, new difficulties to overcome, new
Madonnas to invent, new ideals to imagine.

There will be perhaps photograph Raphaels,
photograph Titians, founders of new empires and
not subverters of the old."

This reasonable endorsement did not succeed in
paving the way for acceptance by the
establishment. Photography was refused a place in
the International Exhibition of 1862 - it could not
be called Fine Art, the judges declared - and there
were bitter criticisms that artists were being
distracted from their main task, to examine, study

and record nature with their own eyes, not with
some new-fangled contraption.

One of the coolest, most sensible judgements
came from Lord Robert Cecil, later the Prime
Minister Lord Salisbury.

In 1864 he rounded on the Luddites and
declared: "Bad artists have lavished upon
photography a good deal of the contempt which,
some 30 years ago, coach-proprietors used to
expend upon the dangerous and inconvenient
system of travelling by railway."

Despite the opprobrium, photography was
evolving all the time. The Calotype had been
superseded, the technical quality of pictures was
becoming crisper and popular photography
already had a firm foothold on the Victorian
scene.

By now the initial enchantment which had
encouraged such careful compositions and
beautifully considered re-workings of the painters'
themes had worn off. Many of the original gifted
amateurs had quit the field and handed over to
the professionals.

The debate still rumbled as the century wore
on. The most self-consciously "artistic"
photographer of all, the visionary Henry Peach
Robinson (1830-1901), who found huge success
with his vast tableaux of carefully composed
figures, rural idylls and engaging portraits of
country girls was quick to spring to
photography's defence. "It requires a fifth-rate
painter to treat photography with contempt", he
robustly declared.

But admirable though Peach Robinson's
pictures are - and some are masterpieces - he was
a rare survivor of that highbrow spirit which had
confused painting with photography. The more
forward-looking, including the author of that
editorial in the RPS Journal, saw that
photography had the potential of an art form in
its own right.

Opposite: Mediterranean romance with a young
couple gaily attired - and looking rather self-conscious
- in Spanish fancy dress. Photography was quick to
exploit the British public's fascination for the exotic, yet
another theme borrowed from art.

Photo: Bristol Records Office

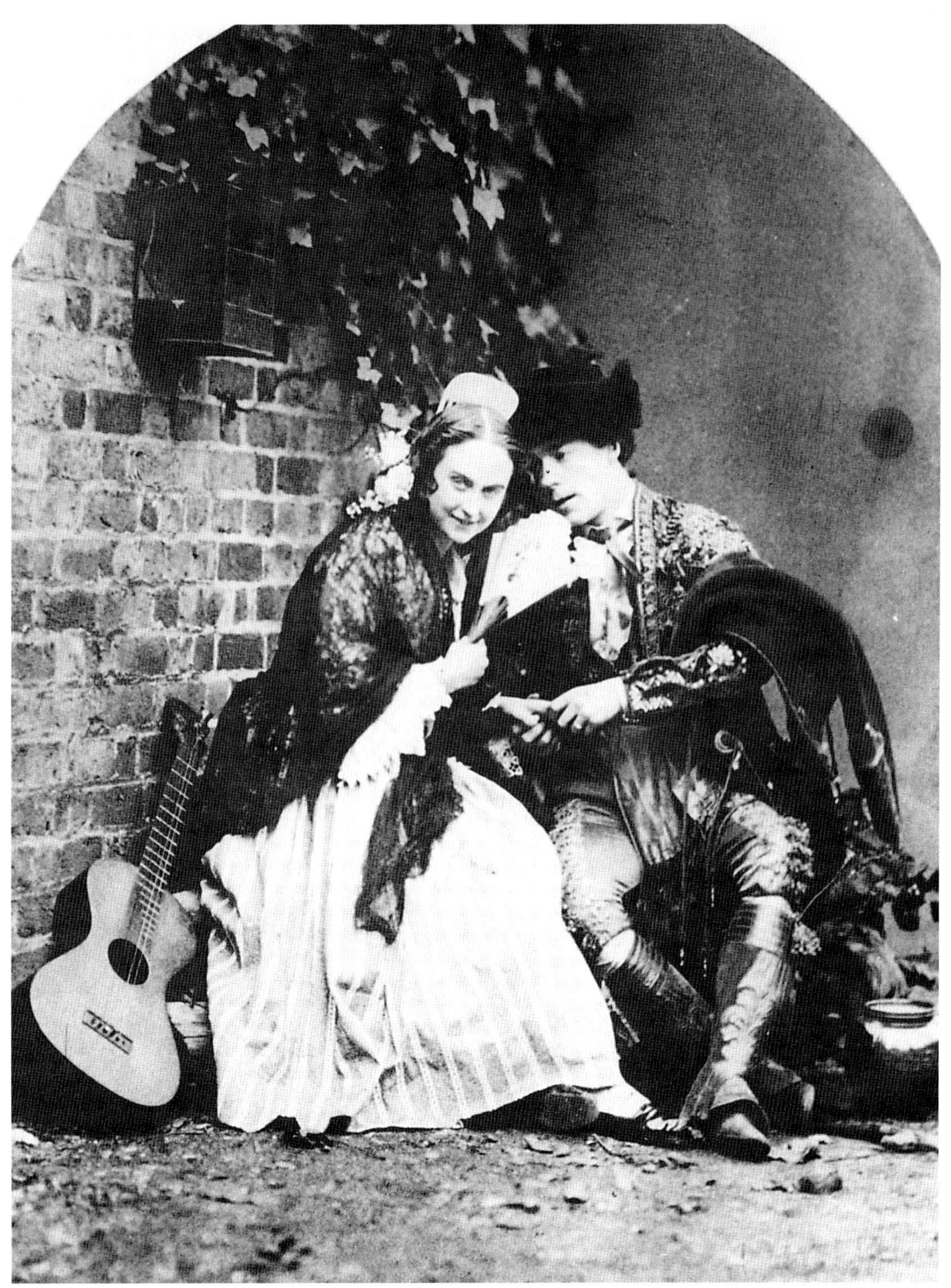

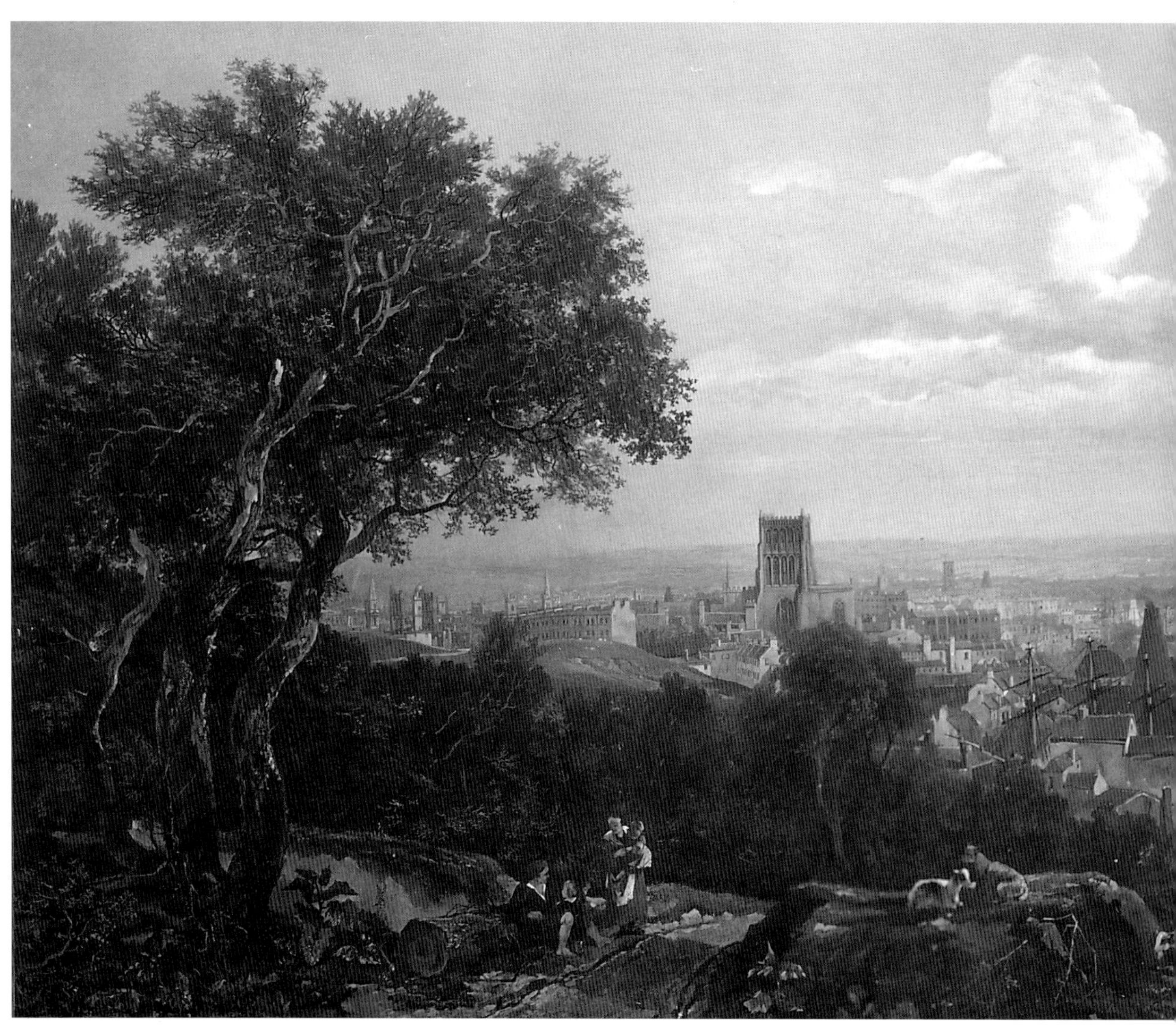

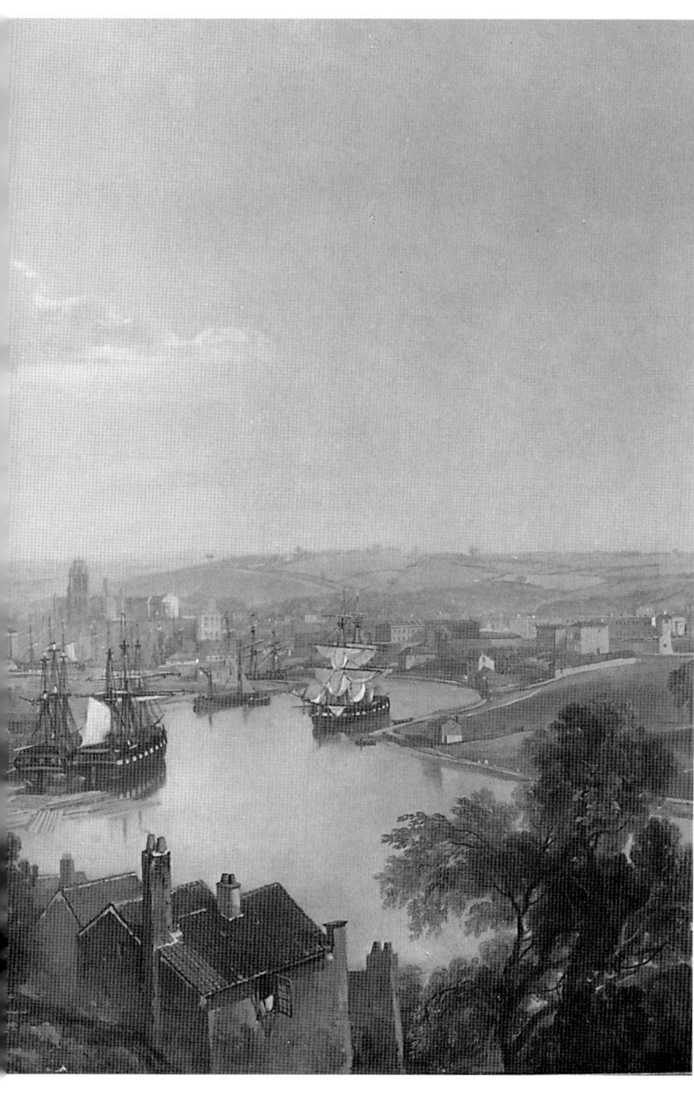

Bristol From Clifton Wood c 1837 by W.J. Muller (1812-1845). This superb panorama stretches from the knot of city church on the left to the new church of St. Paul, Bedminster, beyond the New Gaol on the right. To the right of the Cathedral is the Limekiln Lane glasshouse with the domed building of the Bristol and Clifton Oil Gas Company.

Beyond is the newly extended Bush Warehouse on Narrow Quay below St. Mary Redcliffe. Even the tilt of Temple Church is carefully recorded. However the lichen-covered oaks and sandy soil of the foreground owe more to Dutch 17th century painting than the real Clifton Wood.

Painting: Bristol Museums and Gallery

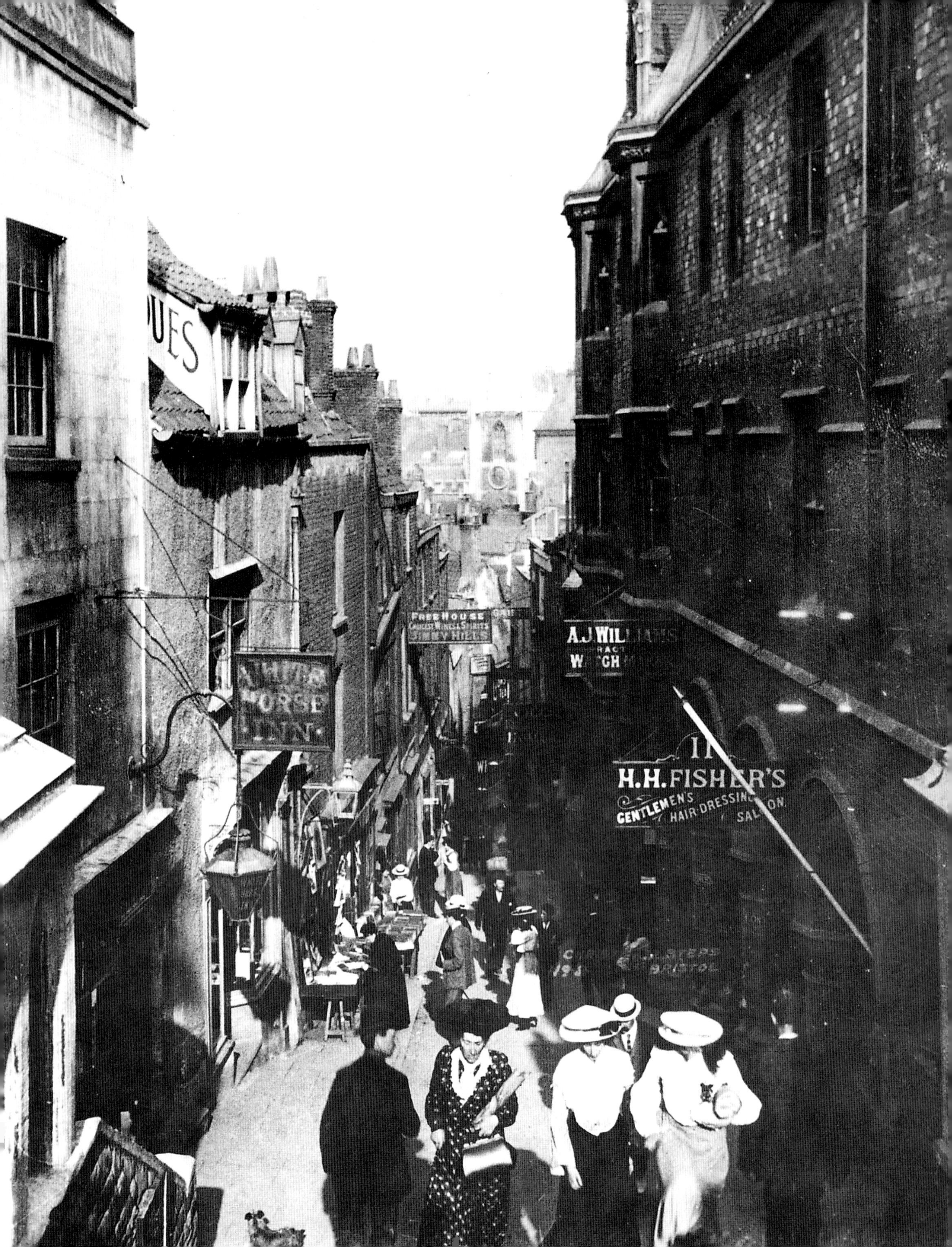
UES
FREE HOUSE
FINEST WINES & SPIRITS
SIMEY HILLS
A.J. WILLIAMS
WATCH M
H.H. FISHER'S
GENTLEMEN'S HAIR-DRESSING SALOON
HORSE INN

The far-sighted Lord Salisbury again touched the truth of the matter. Musing on what would happen when and if colour ever came to photography he wrote:

"The camera would have undisputed possession of all actual scenes and existing objects, and the easel and canvas would be restricted exclusively to imaginative painting."

It is 130 years since Lord Salisbury made his judgement, 140 years since Hugh Owen took his final photographs and more than 150 years since the first photographs were taken in Bristol.

If Owen and friends could return to Bristol today, they would be delighted. Arguments pitting Art against Photography were settled generations ago and photography has found its own natural place with the best photographers hailed as great artists.

Photography is widely exhibited in Bristol. The Watershed media centre stages monthly shows. The Arnolfini gallery regularly features pictures by the world's leading photographers. The City Museum and Art Gallery has held many photographic exhibitions over the years.

They would be amused by the controversy currently raging in the world of photography over digital computer processes which make it possible utterly to transform original images and wrest much of the control from the photographer and hand it to technicians.

In their day the burning issue had been: Is it Art? Today the question has become: Is it Photography?

They would be flattered that Bristol's most internationally famous artist of the 1990s is one of their fraternity. He is Richard Long, winner of the Turner Prize, Britain's top award for a modern artist, and he is a photographer/sculptor . . . the inheritor of a tradition going back to Owen and his friends and the Bristol School of Artists before them.

Richard Long's inspiration as a teenaged artist was the Bristol landscape. He roamed the Downs, Leigh Woods and the Avon Gorge... so the story comes full circle.

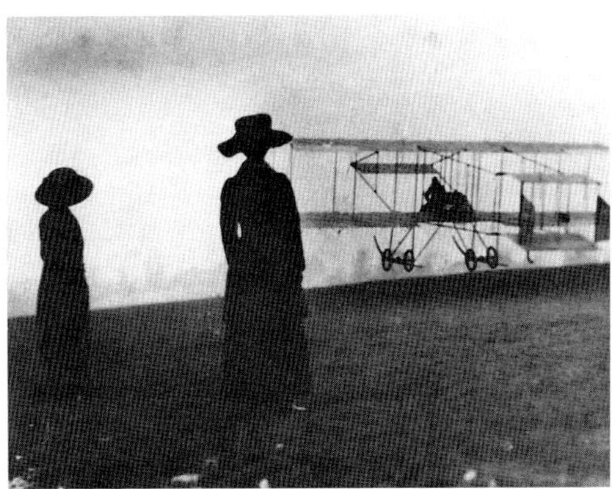

Above: The famous French airman Maurice Tetard takes off in a Bristol Boxkite from the Downs in 1910 before climbing to 100 feet, circling and landing . . . this focused study using a tripod-mounted camera shows the ingenuity of one Edwardian photographer, who must have carefully calculated the point where the plane would leave the ground and found two perfectly placed onlookers to give a sense of scale and drama.

Photo: Bristol Museums and Art Gallery

Opposite: Christmas Steps photographed at the turn of the century. The early, painfully slow exposures demanded by the original Calotype process had now been replaced by rapid exposure film . . . at last Bristol streets could be shown peopled by milling crowds.

Photo: Bristol Museums and Art Gallery

Acknowledgements:

Design of book and exhibition: **Patrick Harrison**

Project co-ordinator: **Paul Elkin,** Bristol Museums and Art Gallery

Photographic reproduction: **Mike Pugh**

Technical/photographic advice: **Dr Graham Reeves FRPS**

Exhibition team for Cartwrights: **Christopher Eskell, Christopher Mitchell** and **Anne Tryggeset**

Selection of paintings: **Francis Greenacre,** Curator of Fine Art, Bristol Museums and Art Gallery

The staff of the Bristol Records Office

Bibliography:

The Bristol School of Artists: Francis Danby and Painting in Bristol 1810-1840 by Francis Greenacre (City of Bristol Art Gallery 1973)

Francis Danby 1793-1861 by Francis Greenacre (Tate Gallery in association with the City of Bristol Museum and Art Gallery 1988)

The Bristol Landscape by Francis Greenacre and Sheena Stoddard (City of Bristol Museum and Art Gallery 1986)

Victorian Painters by Jeremy Maas (Barrie Cresset 1969)

Victoriana by James Laver (Ward Lock 1966)

Victorian Taste by John Steegman (1950, republished by Century in association with the National Trust, 1987)

Bristol As It Was 1845-1900 by Reece Winstone (Reece Winstone 1983)

Bristol's Earliest Photographs by Reece Winstone (Reece Winstone 1974)

Bristol In The 1850s by Reece Winstone (Reece Winstone 1978)

An Early Victorian Album: The Hill/Adamson Collection by Colin Ford and Roy Strong (Jonathan Cape 1974)

Images Of Bristol by James Belsey and David Harrison (Redcliffe Press 1987)

Coleridge: Early Visions by Richard Holmes (Hodder and Stoughton 1989)

Brunel's Bristol by R.A. Buchanan and M. Williams (Redcliffe Press 1982)

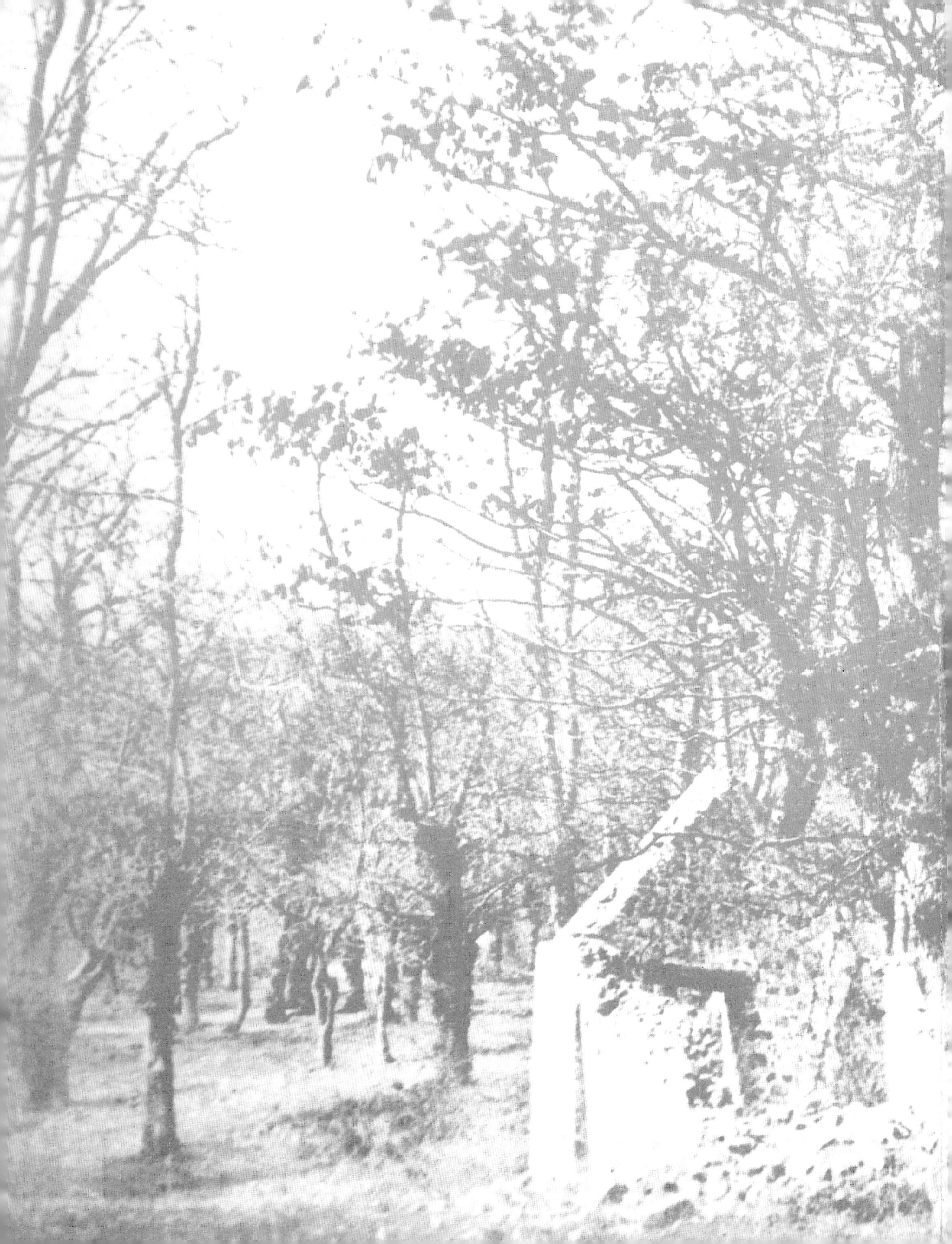